Beyond TRUE STORIES

A HIGH-INTERMEDIATE READER

by Sandra Heyer

Longman

For John
If someone asked me the question on page 65, I would still say, "You."

Beyond True Stories: A High-Intermediate Reader

Pearson Education, 10 Bank Street, White Plains, NY 10606

Acquisitions editor: Laura Le Dréan
Development editor: Stacey Hunter
Vice president, director of design and production: Rhea Banker
Executive managing editor: Linda Moser
Senior production manager: Ray Keating
Production editor: Kathleen Silloway
Director of manufacturing: Patrice Fraccio
Senior manufacturing buyer: Dave Dickey
Cover and text design: Elizabeth Carlson
Cover photo: © Masterfile/Philip Rostron
Text composition: Rainbow Graphics
Text font: 10/12 Aster and 10/12 Frutiger Bold
Text credits: pages 161–162
Photo credits: page 163

Library of Congress Cataloging-in-Publication Data

Heyer, Sandra.
    Beyond true stories / Sandra Heyer.
        p. cm.
    ISBN 0-13-091814-8 (pbk. : alk. paper)
    1. English language—Textbooks for foreign speakers. 2. Readers. I. Title.

PE1128 .H43547 2003
428.6'4—dc21   2002035650

ISBN: 0-13-091814-8 (Student Book)
       0-13-189274-6 (Student Book with CD)

LONGMAN ON THE **WEB**

Longman.com offers online resources for teachers and students. Access our Companion Websites, our online catalog, and our local offices around the world.

Visit us at **longman.com**.

Printed in the United States of America
9 10 11 12 13 14 V004 14 13 12 11 10

Contents

Scope & Sequence

READING SKILLS	VOCABULARY DEVELOPMENT
Identifying main ideas • Identifying supporting ideas • Understanding an idea map • Recognizing supporting evidence • Reading a chart	Using context clues Building academic vocabulary
Sequencing events • Understanding cause and effect • Summarizing • Identifying main ideas • Reading a chart	Understanding special expressions Identifying the right definition
Paraphrasing main ideas • Scanning • Making inferences • Responding to the reading • Recognizing details • Reading a bar graph	Understanding special expressions Understanding academic vocabulary Understanding slang expressions
Paraphrasing main ideas • Understanding story setting • Making inferences • Separating fact from opinion • Reading a bar graph	Using new words Building academic vocabulary
Paraphrasing main ideas • Scanning for information • Understanding chronological order • Reading actively • Reading a pie chart	Understanding special expressions Building academic vocabulary
Visualizing a scene • Using a time line • Understanding cause and effect • Paraphrasing main ideas	Recognizing related words Understanding academic vocabulary Understanding legal terms
Understanding cause and effect • Identifying main ideas and supporting details • Paraphrasing • Reading a bar graph	Using new words Understanding specialized terms
Identifying main ideas • Understanding time expressions • Making inferences • Making an outline • Reading a graph	Using new words Understanding academic vocabulary Understanding field-specific terms

To the Teacher

Beyond True Stories is an intermediate to high-intermediate reading textbook for students of English. It is fundamentally a reading text, but its ample discussion and writing exercises make it also well suited for integrated-skills courses, such as those that combine instruction in reading, writing, and speaking. For most courses, the text will provide material for a semester's instruction.

The book consists of eight thematically linked units. The themes are intentionally narrow. Narrow topics ensure that the same words and expressions recycle from reading to reading. Students have the vocabulary they need to respond to the topics in discussions and in writing and the practice necessary to retain it.

Beyond True Stories has been designed so that each unit stands alone. The To the Student section is a distinctive feature of this book. Here students are invited to read the units in any order, beginning with the stories and topics that interest them most. Giving students the freedom and power to make this choice can transform a class. If your curriculum allows some flexibility, please try this approach. In small classes, students can decide by consensus where they would like to begin; in larger classes, they can vote. To accommodate students' skipping from topic to topic, the units are freestanding; students' success in later units is not contingent on their having completed earlier units.

Within each unit, there are six sections:

A True Story in the News The first reading in each unit is a human-interest story adapted from contemporary news sources, such as newspapers, magazines, and TV interviews. These high-interest readings pique students' interest in the topic and introduce vocabulary that recurs throughout the unit. A True Story in the News opens with an authentic photo and pre-reading questions that encourage students to make predictions about the reading. Immediately following the story is a short comprehension exercise called Getting the Big Picture. This exercise tests students' global understanding of the story. Students then proceed to exercises that build vocabulary, reading skills, and critical thinking skills. Readers will notice that this section has the format and spirit of the other books in the True Stories series.

A Personal Story The personal story is a first-person account of someone who has had an experience related to the theme of the unit. Because these personal stories are authentic, with only minor simplifications, students may find some readings quite challenging. Teachers may wish to adjust the task to the complexity of the reading, perhaps by asking students to strive for a thorough understanding of some readings but to read others for the main ideas only. Each personal story is followed by Sharing Your True Stories, in which students are invited to share their own true stories related to the unit theme.

News and Views This section contains an expository reading. The intention of this section is to prepare students for the type of material they encounter in textbooks. Some of the News and Views readings are authentic, and some are adapted. (You can tell authentic from adapted readings this way: Authentic readings carry the byline of the writer, whereas adapted readings are not identified by author.) Each reading is followed by exercises that develop vocabulary and reading skills. Most of the vocabulary exercises in this section target words that were drawn from the Academic Word List. The list, developed by Averil Coxhead, consists of ten sublists containing the most commonly used academic vocabulary. For an explanation and the complete list, see Appendix 3.

Reading a Graphic In this section, students practice reading bar graphs, line graphs, pie charts, maps, and lists. The graphic is followed by a list of discussion questions that encourage students to think critically about the information in the graphic.

Discussion This section consists not only of discussion questions but also of interactive activities that promote discussion. The activities can be done in pairs, in small groups, or as a class. (To ensure that everyone takes part in small-group discussions, you may wish to appoint a discussion leader for each group. It is the leader's job to make sure that the discussion moves along and that everyone has the opportunity to participate.) Occasionally, students are asked to check the answers to questions they have discussed in Appendix 2: Checking Your Answers.

Writing This section offers a choice of writing prompts. The whole class can write on the same topic, or students can choose to write about the topic that interests them most. If the whole class is writing on the same topic, you may wish to try this procedure:

- Explain to the students exactly what the assignment calls for. (For example, "Your essay should have details that help the reader imagine your experience.")

- Give students a model essay to read. This essay should clearly exemplify the characteristics that are to be modeled.

- Help the students pinpoint why the model essay serves as a good example.

Research in writing indicates that this three-step preparation for writing—description, model, explication—helps students become more aware of writing methods and does not hinder their creativity. It is important, of course, to have models that are accessible to students; one source of models is the writing of former students. Initially, you will have no sample essays (unless you write them yourself), but if you save superior writing samples each semester, you will acquire a collection of model essays. (Ask students to write "OK to use" at the top of essays they are comfortable sharing and emphasize that their essays will be used only as examples of superior writing.)

Grading ESL writing—especially writing about personal experiences—can be difficult. One way to grade student writing is to base the grade on a set of eight to ten criteria you give the students before they write. For example, if the students' task is to describe a personal experience, one of the criteria might be that their essay have three details that help the reader imagine the experience. Or the criteria might target grammatical points you have been working on. You could specify, for example, that the essay use correct forms of past-tense verbs. Assign each criterion a certain point value and grade the essay, at least in part, on whether it meets the criteria.

Developing Reading Skills

Each unit has two sets of exercises that help students develop their reading skills. These exercises target more than 20 reading skills, such as previewing, predicting, scanning, making inferences, and understanding the main ideas. The exercises serve two purposes:

1. *They test comprehension.* Some students say that they often understand every word in a reading but don't understand what the reading is actually about. Immigrant students in particular—who may have lived in an English-speaking country for years—complain that lack of real comprehension is their biggest reading problem. If a comprehension exercise reveals that students do not understand the main ideas of a reading, advise them to go back to the reading and try to figure out where they went astray. Students will sometimes make comments such as "I was reading too fast" or "I always thought the main idea came in the first paragraph, but here it didn't." More often than not, students can put themselves on the road to better comprehension.

2. *They help students develop reading skills and strategies that they can use throughout their reading careers.* Reading is an invisible process. Teachers cannot observe students as they are reading and say, "Yes! You're doing it exactly right!" But they can do two things: (1) Provide students with reading material that interests them and is at the appropriate level. (2) Introduce them to new strategies that will help them become better readers, as well as make them aware of effective strategies they are already using. The goal of *Beyond True Stories* is to help you do both of the above.

Feel free to adjust all of the exercises to suit yourself and to suit your students. If an exercise in one unit is particularly helpful, repeat it in other units. Skip an exercise that is too easy or too hard, or modify it. Turn writing prompts into discussion questions, and turn discussion questions into writing prompts. Please give yourself free rein to experiment with other aspects of the book as well. If you spot your students peeking ahead to the graph instead of reading the story, read the graph before the story. Let your students go where their interests take them, and be prepared for surprises.

The goal of this book—and of all the books in the True Stories series—is to make reading easier for your students and to make teaching easier for you. Above all, it is hoped that reading *Beyond True Stories* will be a pleasure, for both you and your students.

Acknowledgments

I wish to thank the following people who assisted in field testing:
Christine LeCloux and her students at REEP (Arlington Education and Employment Program), Arlington, VA; **Peggy Miles** and her students at the Santa Cruz Adult School, Santa Cruz, CA; **Setsuko Toyama,** who field-tested the story "Chosen" with students and teachers in Japan and who provided invaluable feedback; **students at the University of Wisconsin,** Whitewater, and Whitewater High School students **Maria Arzate, Amador Cortez,** and **Alejandro Angel;** and **Zsofi Hegyi.**

I also wish to thank **Laura Le Dréan,** my patient editor at Longman; **Stacey Hunter** at Longman, who helped me use these stories to their fullest potential; **Mindy Hohenstein,** who assisted in research; **Nancy Hayward,** Indiana University of Pennsylvania, who read early drafts of the stories; **Susan Huss-Lederman,** University of Wisconsin, Whitewater, who introduced me to the method of grading ESL essays that is suggested in the To the Teacher section; **Ben Rafoth,** Indiana University of Pennsylvania, whose syllabus inspired the organization of the Contents; **Lori Hohenstein,** who told me about the story "Shipmates and Soul Mates"; **Bob Pagani** and **Tom Kraemer,** who shared the story of Tom's "Dream Girl"; and **Irvin Scott,** who provided the first-hand account of the experiences on which "Chosen" was based.

The author and publisher would like to thank the following reviewers, who offered invaluable insights and suggestions for *Beyond True Stories*: **Nanette Dougherty,** UFT Teacher Center, Jackson Heights, NY; **Serkan Gülsen,** Yeditepe University, Istanbul, Turkey; **Matthew Huseby,** McHenry County College, Crystal Lake, IL; **Jim Kahny,** Language Institute of Japan, Odawara, Kanagawa, Japan; **Christine LeCloux,** REEP, Clarendon Education Center, Arlington, VA; **José Napoleón Quintero Nieto,** Centro Internacional de Educación y Desarrollo, Filial de Petroleos de Venezuela; **Marta Pitt,** Lindsey Hopkins Technical Education Center, Miami, FL; **Mary Segovia,** El Monte/Rosemead Adult School, Rosemead, CA; and **Abigail Tom,** Durham Technical Community College, Durham, NC.

To the Student

You can read the stories in this book in the traditional order—that is, you can begin with Unit 1 and finish with Unit 8. Or, if your teacher agrees, you can skip around and read the stories that interest you most first. If your teacher and class choose to do this, read these short descriptions of each unit. Then, with your class, decide which topics interest you most and which unit you would like to read first.

Unit 1

This man lives in a village in Italy where people live to be very old—85, 95, and even older. What is their secret? Do you want to live to be 100? A doctor gives his advice for living a long and healthy life.

Unit 2

On September 11, 2001, while everyone was running out of the World Trade Center in New York City, this firefighter ran into the building. He risked his life doing what he loves to do: fight fires. How do you find the work that is right for you—work that you love doing?

Unit 3

These two men are fascinated by the Internet and have a talent for working with computers. That talent brought them phenomenal success. Do you think a certain type of person is attracted to technology? Are you that kind of person?

Unit 4

These two couples found love on a cruise ship. Are you looking for love? What kind of person are you looking for? Learn what young people in different countries are looking for in a husband or wife.

Unit 5

This woman used her intuition to find a dinosaur skeleton. What exactly is intuition? How can you use intuition to help you in your own life?

Unit 6

This family fought with another family for years. Their feud is the most famous in American history. How did their fight start? How did it end? Have you ever had a problem with a neighbor? Learn what the most common neighborhood problems are and how to solve them.

Unit 7

This woman made $22 million by investing in the stock market. How did she do it? Can anyone do what she did? Learn some quick tips for investing in the stock market.

Unit 8

This man is alive because a stranger risked his life to save him. Why did the stranger do that? Why do people help one another? One explanation for helping behavior may surprise you.

Longevity

The theme of this unit is longevity—a long life. How long is "a long life"?
How old is "old"? Are you old when you turn 50 . . . or 60 . . . or 75 . . . or 80?

In your opinion, at what age does a person become "old"? Write the age here: _____

Now, read your number aloud and listen as your classmates read their numbers aloud. Then discuss the answers to these questions with your classmates.

1. Why did you write the number you did? Why do you think someone becomes old at that age?

2. Do your classmates agree on what is old? That is, did most people write numbers that are close to one another? If there is a big difference between the lowest number and the highest number, what could explain the difference?

3. Can you notice any patterns in the numbers people chose? For example, did older classmates write higher numbers than younger classmates? Did classmates from the same part of the world write numbers that are close to one another?

In this unit, you will read about some people who are very old. First, you will read about a village in Italy where people often live to be 90, and even older. Then you will read the personal story of Sadie Delany, who lived to be 109. Finally, you will read a doctor's advice on how you can have a long, sweet life.

PRE-READING

Look at the photo and read the title of the story on page 3. Then think about these questions. Discuss your answers with your classmates.

▶ The man in the photo likes to ride his bright blue moped up and down the mountainous roads near his town. Can you guess how old he is? Look on page 154 to find out.

▶ The man lives in Campodimele, a village in Italy where people live to be very old. It is rare for anyone to die before the age of 85, and most people stay healthy and busy well into their 90s. What do you think might be some reasons for their health and longevity?

With your classmates, make a list of possible reasons people stay healthy and live long in Campodimele. Then read the story to find out what researchers concluded.

La Dolce Vita (The Sweet Life)

1   When he was 34 years old, Gerardo Pecchia left his village in Italy to work in the United States. He worked in the United States for 40 years; then, at the age of 74, he retired and returned to Campodimele, his native village.

2   Campodimele was as beautiful as Gerardo remembered it. The tiny town is on a mountaintop 75 miles south of Rome, surrounded by olive trees. A medieval wall encircles the village, and narrow stone streets wind between its quaint old houses. In the center of the town there is a picturesque *piazza*—a town square—where people gather to chat in the shade of a 300-year-old elm tree. Even the weather in Campodimele is beautiful: At 2,100 feet above sea level, the town catches fresh sea breezes that keep the temperatures moderate—not too hot, and not too cold.

3   Gerardo was happy to be back in Campodimele among family and old friends. He was happy, too, that he had enough money to enjoy his retirement. During his 40 years in the United States, he had paid into the Social Security fund, so he received a small pension. Each time he cashed a check, he exchanged his U.S. dollars for Italian lira, and he had enough lira to live a simple but comfortable life.

4   Gerardo lived contentedly in Campodimele for 25 years; then, when he was 99 years old, he had a serious problem—not with his health, as could be expected at that age—but with the U.S. government. Officials at the U.S. Embassy in Rome noticed that a 99-year-old man named Gerardo Pecchia was cashing Social Security checks in Campodimele. They had a hard time believing that Gerardo Pecchia could still be alive. Perhaps he had died, they thought, and a son or nephew with the same name was illegally cashing the checks. Embassy officials wrote Mr. Pecchia, asking for proof that he was alive. Gerardo traveled to Rome and went to the embassy in person. "I am Gerardo Pecchia," he told the officials there. "As you can see, I am still alive."

5   Gerardo Pecchia was not just alive—he was alive and well. He was still taking care of his garden, still doing his own shopping, still taking the bus to visit his son. Anywhere else in the world, people would be amazed to see a 99-year-old man with such vitality. In Campodimele, however, it is not a surprising sight. In the tiny town of 890 people, 48 are over the age of 90, and most of them, like Gerardo, are healthy and busy. They chop wood, milk cows, and hunt; they take care of gardens and olive trees. One 94-year-old man is often seen riding his bright blue moped on the mountainous roads around Campodimele.

6   When Gerardo retired in Campodimele, he retired in one of the healthiest places on earth. It is rare for anybody in Campodimele to die before reaching the age of 85, and people remain healthy and active well into their 90s. In 1985, the World Health Organization sent a team of medical researchers to Campodimele. Their task was to determine why people there lived such long and healthy lives. The researchers discovered that the blood pressure of elderly Campodimeleans was exceptionally low. It was not unusual for a 90-year-old man to have the same blood pressure level as his 20-year-old great-grandson. Cholesterol levels were low, too—around 100, less than half the usual level in most Western nations. These findings fascinated the researchers. If Campodimeleans can have such low blood pressure and cholesterol levels, why can't we all? What is their secret? Is it diet? Is it lifestyle? Or is it simply good genes?

(continued)

7   Some residents of Campodimele credit the water they drink for their longevity and health. For centuries the village has been known for its mineral water, which people collect from several fountains in the town. People claim the minerals in the water prevent hardening of the arteries. Other residents credit the food they eat for their good health. The people of Campodimele eat a traditional Mediterranean diet, which consists mainly of fresh vegetables, pasta, wild mushrooms, olive oil, shallots, and a moderate amount of red wine. They eat very little meat, salt, or butter, and very few people in the village are heavy coffee drinkers, unlike other Italians. A typical lunch in Campodimele might be homemade bread grilled with olive oil and tomatoes; spaghetti with carrots, onions, and tomatoes; and perhaps some seafood, snails fried in olive oil, or local beans, called *cicerchie*.

8   The researchers wondered if the lifestyle in Campodimele could be having a positive effect on residents' health, so they observed people as they went about their daily lives. The researchers concluded that the lifestyle did have a positive effect. In Campodimele, most people follow a traditional rural timetable: They get up at sunrise, go to bed at 8 P.M., and eat at the same time every day. They also get plenty of exercise. Because the streets are so narrow, walking is the usual way to get around Campodimele. Nearly everyone works daily in gardens or takes care of chickens or other small animals. Many of Campodimele's inhabitants are farmers, and they keep fit walking up and down the steep hillside that separates the village from their plots of land. In addition, the lifestyle seems, at least on the surface, to be free of stress. There is no crime in Campodimele, and there is no traffic because cars are not allowed in the center of the village. Perhaps most important, elderly people are not separated from younger people; they do not live in retirement homes but instead are well integrated with the rest of the population. In Campodimele, it is not unusual to see four generations gather to chat under the elm tree in the piazza. Dr. Pietro Cugini, who led the research, noted: "The elderly person is never alone, but has a life synchronized with that of others, as in one big family."

9   In addition to examining the water, diet, and lifestyle in Campodimele, the researchers tried to determine if the longevity of Campodimeleans, who have been members of only a few families for centuries, has a genetic cause. Dr. Cugini believes that genes do play a role. Many inhabitants have a special enzyme that reduces blood pressure and cholesterol levels. Moreover, a study of Campodimeleans who left the village for Toronto, Canada, in the 1960s showed that they, too, lived long and healthy lives—an indication that Campodimeleans carry a gene for longevity. Still, Dr. Cugini does not think that good genes alone guarantee longevity. "You also need a well-structured lifestyle," he warns. At the end of the four-year study, he concluded that the villagers' health and longevity are based 30 percent on genetics and 70 percent on environment.

10   The old people in Campodimele seemed puzzled by all the laboratory tests and record-keeping. Pasquale Pannozzi, 83, wondered, "I don't know why they are spending all this time in Campodimele. The answer is easy: This is a perfect spot. No stress. Who would want to die?" ◆

GETTING THE BIG PICTURE

Circle the letter of your answer.

Why do the people of Campodimele have unusually long and healthy lives?

a. They have a healthy diet, a healthy lifestyle, and good genes. The fact that Campodimele is beautiful—"a perfect spot"—probably helps, too.

b. Fresh sea breezes keep the air clean. Although the town is only 75 miles from Rome, there is no pollution.

c. Doctors from the World Health Organization have been living in Campodimele since 1985, studying the people. Campodimeleans have the best medical care in the world.

BUILDING VOCABULARY

◆ RECALLING NEW WORDS

The words below are from the story. Write the correct word or words on each line.

had a hard time	amazed	retire	vitality
native village	pension	rural	puzzled
wind (verb)		proof	

1. Gerardo Pecchia was born in a small town in Italy, but he went to the United States when he was 34. Forty years later, he returned to his

   _____.

2. Most people stop working when they are 65, but Gerardo didn't

   _____ until he was 74.

3. Gerardo paid taxes when he worked in the United States, so when he retired, he received a little money every month from the U.S. government. His

   _____ was small, but he had enough money to live comfortably.

4. It was difficult for the embassy officials to believe that a 99-year-old man was still cashing Social Security checks. They _____ believing that Mr. Pecchia was still alive.

5. Embassy officials wanted Mr. Pecchia to show them that he was still living: They wanted to see papers or other information. They wanted

   _____ that he was alive.

6. Gerardo had a lot of energy: He was taking care of his garden, doing his own shopping, and taking the bus to visit his son. Like many old people in Campodimele, he had great _____.

7. In Campodimele, people are not surprised when they see 90-year-olds hunting and chopping wood. In other places in the world, however, people would be so surprised, they would find it hard to believe. They would be _____ to see it.

8. Campodimele sits on the top of a mountain, so its streets cannot be straight. They go around the mountain and _____ between the houses.

9. Many of the people in Campodimele are farmers, and almost everyone has a garden or small animals. Campodimele is in a _____ part of Italy.

10. The old people in Campodimele didn't understand why the researchers wanted to study them. They were _____ by all the laboratory tests and record-keeping.

◆ USING CONTEXT CLUES

> Sometimes you can find the meaning of a word or phrase from the context clues—the surrounding words and sentences. Before looking up a word in a dictionary, check for context clues.

In each sentence, circle the word or words that have the same meaning as the words in italics. The first one is done for you.

1. In the center of the town, there is a *piazza*—a town square—where people gather.

2. Campodimele has *moderate temperatures*—not too hot and not too cold.

3. Gerardo was happy and satisfied because his life was good in Campodimele. He was *contented* there.

4. A typical lunch in Campodimele might be homemade bread; spaghetti with carrots, onions, and tomatoes; and perhaps some seafood or local beans, called *cicerchie.*

5. In Italy, there are people who drink a lot of coffee, but the people in Campodimele are not *heavy coffee drinkers.*

6. The researchers wondered if the lifestyle in Campodimele could be having a positive effect on *residents'* health, so they observed the people living there as they went about their daily lives.

7. Elderly people are not separated from younger people; they are well *integrated* with the rest of the population.

8. Researchers wondered if genes have an influence on Campodimeleans' longevity. They discovered that genes do *play a role.*

DEVELOPING READING SKILLS

◆ UNDERSTANDING THE MAIN IDEAS

There are three correct ways to complete each sentence. Draw a line through the one incorrect answer.

1. Campodimele
   a. is a tiny town on a mountaintop 75 miles from Rome.
   b. ~~was the birthplace of many famous Italians.~~
   c. is a beautiful town that has beautiful weather.
   d. is one of the healthiest places on earth.

2. The people of Campodimele
   a. rarely die before age 85.
   b. travel to Canada for medical care.
   c. remain healthy and active well into their 90s.
   d. have low blood pressure and low cholesterol levels.

3. The medical researchers who went to Campodimele
   a. were sent by the World Health Organization.
   b. tried to determine why people in Campodimele lived such long and healthy lives.
   c. observed people as they went about their daily lives.
   d. concluded that the lifestyle in Campodimele did not have a positive effect on residents' health.

4. The doctor who led the research in Campodimele
   a. noticed that elderly people are never alone.
   b. believes that good genes guarantee longevity.
   c. believes people need a well-structured lifestyle.
   d. concluded that Campodimeleans' health and longevity are based 30 percent on genetics and 70 percent on environment.

◆ UNDERSTANDING SUPPORTING IDEAS

The ability to understand which information supports a main idea is an important reading skill. Sentences with supporting ideas give you more information about the main ideas, often by explaining or giving examples. For example, look at paragraph 2 of *"La Dolce Vita"* on page 3. The main idea of the paragraph—that Campodimele is beautiful—is followed by many supporting ideas: "The tiny town is . . . surrounded by olive trees . . . narrow stone streets wind between its quaint old houses. In the center of the town there is a picturesque *piazza*—a town square."

Read each sentence below. Then write a sentence that gives more information. Write your answer on the line. The first two are done for you.

1. Gerardo Pecchia was alive and well. *He was still taking care of his garden, still doing his own shopping, and still taking the bus to visit his son.*

2. Some Campodimeleans credit the water they drink for their longevity. *It contains minerals which may prevent hardening of the arteries.*

3. Campodimeleans eat a traditional Mediterranean diet. _____
_____

4. Most people follow a traditional rural timetable. _____
_____

5. Campodimeleans get plenty of exercise. _____
_____

6. The lifestyle seems free of stress. _____
_____

◆ **UNDERSTANDING AN IDEA MAP**

An *idea map* presents the main ideas and the supporting ideas of a reading in a visual way. Drawing an idea map after you read helps you recognize how a reading is organized and helps you remember the main ideas.

Look at the idea map below, which represents the organization of the story "La Dolce Vita." Some information is missing from the map. Write the missing information on each line.

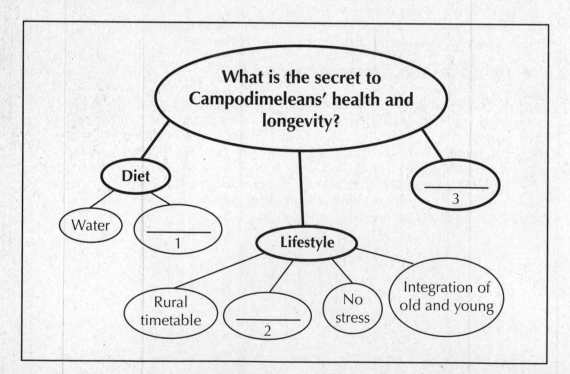

In 1993, two sisters named Bessie and Sadie Delany, ages 101 and 103, published their memoir—a collection of their memories. Their book *Having Our Say* became a best-seller in the United States, and the Delany sisters were instantly famous. In the chapter below, Sadie tells what it's like to be more than 100 years old. She died six years after she wrote these words, at age 109.

Before you read, think about this: What do you think Sadie's life is like? Do you think, for example, that she uses a wheelchair or that she sleeps most of the time? Imagine what life could be like for someone who is 103. Then read Sadie's description of her everyday life.

From *Having Our Say* by Sadie and Bessie Delany

We both forget we're old. This happens all the time. I'll reach for something real quick, just like a young person. And I realize my reflexes are not what they once were. It surprises me, but I can't complain. I still do what I want, pretty much.

These days, I am usually the first one awake in the morning. I wake up at six-thirty. And the first thing I do when I open my eyes is smile, and then I say, "Thank you, Lord, for another day!"

If I don't hear Bessie get up, I'll go into her room and wake her. Sometimes I have to knock on the headboard of her bed. And she opens her eyes and says, "Oh, Lord, another day?!" I don't think Bessie would get up at all sometimes, if it weren't for me. She stays up late in her room and listens to these talk-radio shows, and she doesn't get enough sleep.

In the mornings, Monday through Friday, we do our yoga exercises. I started doing yoga exercises about forty years ago. Well, when Bessie turned eighty she decided that I looked better than her. So she decided she would start doing yoga, too. So we've been doing our exercises together ever since. We follow a yoga exercise program on the TV. Sometimes, Bessie cheats. I'll be doing an exercise and look over at her, and she's just lying there! She's a naughty old gal.

Exercise is very important. A lot of older people don't exercise at all. Another thing that is terribly important is diet. I keep up with the latest news about nutrition. About thirty years ago, Bessie and I started eating much more healthy foods. We don't eat fatty food very often. When we do, we feel like we can't move!

We eat as many as seven different vegetables a day. Plus lots of fresh fruits. And we take vitamin supplements: Vitamin A, B complex, C, D, E, and minerals, too, like zinc.

Every morning, after we do our yoga, we each take a clove of garlic, chop it up, and swallow it. If you swallow it all at once, there is no odor. We also take a teaspoon of cod liver oil. Bessie thinks it's disgusting. But one day I said, "Now, dear little sister, if you want to keep up with me, you're going to have to start taking it, every day, and stop complaining." And she's been good ever since.

These days, I do most of the cooking, and Bessie does the serving. We eat our big meal of the day at noon. In the

(continued)

evening, we usually have a milk shake for dinner, and then we go upstairs and watch the news on the TV.

After that, we say our prayers. We say prayers in the morning and before we go to bed. It takes a long time to pray for everyone, because it's a very big family—we have fifteen nieces and nephews still living, plus all their children and grandchildren. We pray for each one. The ones that Bessie doesn't approve of get extra prayers. Bessie can be very critical and she holds things against people forever. I always have to say to her, "Everybody has to be themselves, Bessie. Live and let live."

You know, when you are this old, you don't know if you're going to wake up in the morning. But I don't worry about dying, and neither does Bessie. We are at peace. You do kind of wonder, when's it going to happen? That's why you learn to love each and every day, child. ◆

◆ SHARING YOUR TRUE STORIES

Discuss the answers to these questions with your classmates.

1. What did Sadie and Bessie do to stay healthy? Make a list.
   For example: *They did yoga.*

   They kept up with the latest news on nutrition.

   Is there anything on the list that you do—or would like to do—so that you can have a long, healthy life?

2. Are there any things Sadie and Bessie did that people in your country usually don't do? Are there any things Sadie and Bessie did that people in your country often do, too?

3. Of all the things Sadie and Bessie did to stay healthy, which do you think are the most important? Why?

4. Does Sadie remind you of someone you know or have known? Tell the class who the person is and why he or she is like Sadie in some way.

NEWS AND VIEWS

How can we have long and healthy lives, like Sadie and Bessie Delany and the people of Campodimele, Italy? Dr. Zorba Paster has some suggestions.

Dr. Paster is a medical doctor and a professor at the University of Wisconsin Medical School. He gives medical advice on a weekly radio show and has written a book called *The Longevity Code*. In his book, Dr. Paster tells us how to have long, healthy lives. His advice is based on scientific research, his own experience as a doctor, and common sense. Here is his "prescription" for a long, sweet life.

Before you begin reading, look at the six subheadings. Each subheading gives you the topic of the paragraphs below it. Notice, too, the illustration of the five interlocking rings. What could be the connection between the rings and the topic of the article—how to have a long, healthy life? (Take a guess, and remember that no logical guess is wrong.)

From *The Longevity Code* by Dr. Zorba Paster

1   Jeanne Calmet, of Arles, France, was still living in her own apartment at age 110. At age 115, she was still riding her bicycle. When she died in 1997 at the age of 122, she had lived longer than any person on record.

2   Perhaps you wouldn't want to live to 122, but certainly you would like to live a long and healthy life. We all want to know the tricks for prolonging our lives, and physicians and researchers have written thousands of pages on the topic. Most of them write about the benefits of taking care of your body: Cut your cholesterol, lose weight, exercise, stop smoking, and watch your blood pressure. While cholesterol, diet, exercise, and not smoking are important, there is more to consider. Just as critical are how much you like your job, whether you have a good relationship with your parents and children, whether you're depressed or happy, angry or delighted, mean or kindhearted.

3   We would all agree that these factors count in quality of life. The fact is that they count in length of life, too—perhaps even as much as the physical factors your doctor can treat. The truth is that being well does not simply mean being in great physical shape. Overall good health is composed of five unique spheres of wellness: the physical, the mental, the family and social, the spiritual, and the material. Picture the Olympic symbol of five interlocking rings. Like the Olympic rings, the five spheres of wellness overlap and interact. Most of us have experienced the way the spheres affect one another. Perhaps mental stress caused a headache, which hurt so much you stayed home from a party, which meant you spent Saturday night alone, which made you so depressed you ate a quart of ice cream. Or perhaps the spheres of wellness interacted in a positive way: A peaceful walk on the beach calmed your mind, relaxed your body, gave you physical exercise, helped you sleep better, made you more pleasant to be around, and so on.

4   In order to live a life that is not only long, but happy, satisfied, and fulfilling—what I call a "sweet" life—you must have good health in all five spheres. Knowing which areas need the most improvement and which are already healthy is the key to increasing your life span.

Sphere #1: Physical

5   There is more to physical health than being "healthy"—that is, not being sick. To increase your chances of having a long life, you also need to pay attention to physical fitness, nutrition, and safety strategies, like wearing a seat belt.

6   Physical fitness is definitely a plus in the physical sphere. Basically, the secret to physical fitness is being active. The more we use our muscles—whether we use them to clean the house or run a marathon—the more physically fit, energetic, and long-lived we're likely to be. Sedentary lifestyles, on the other hand, limit longevity—they're one of the top ten causes of premature death.

Sphere #2: Mental

7   There are a number of psychological illnesses that have a negative impact on

(continued)

longevity. Depression is one of them; severe anxiety is another. So, if you are depressed or very anxious, it's important to find the treatment that will help you.

8   It's also important to control your anger. Becoming furious over every small frustration is truly deadly: Studies indicate that after a fit of anger—especially the face-reddening, fist-clenching, furniture-pounding kind—the risk of having a heart attack is more than twice as high.

9   Finally, it's important to keep your mind sharp and challenged. Lifelong learning is one way to do that. As we age, one of our greatest fears is that our bodies will keep going but our minds will stop working. Lifelong learning keeps our minds active.

Sphere #3: Family and Social

10   A recent study compared the longevity of three groups of people: "couch potatoes" (sedentary types who spent most of their free time watching TV); "gym rats" (people who were compulsive about exercising); and "social butterflies" (people who often got together with other people). Guess which group had the longest and healthiest lives? The social butterflies.

11   Bonds with other people improve our outlook and build self-confidence. Social support also helps us get through stressful times. Those of us who have the support of family and friends are less likely to have heart disease and generally live longer.

Sphere #4: Spiritual

12   Physicians rarely talk about religion; it's a topic that's so personal, it's almost taboo. Yet scientific evidence shows that a spiritual or religious path not only gives comfort but also adds to longevity.

13   The spiritual sphere is the most difficult to describe. It includes anything we do to contemplate the higher meaning and purpose of our lives: meditation, prayer, attending religious services, reading inspirational material, chanting, sitting quietly in a garden, or walking through a forest. And yes, all of this is connected to life expectancy and life quality.

Sphere #5: Material

14   The material sphere is where you find all your "stuff"—all the things outside yourself that affect how you feel. This sphere includes your job, your house, your car, your bank account, and your credit card debt.

15   One part of the material sphere is financial. Having a lot of money is not important, but being content with what you have is. A huge home, luxury cars, and diamonds will not make your life better or help you live longer. However, if not having those things makes you feel ashamed or jealous, then not having what you want could be a problem. Indeed, simply feeling that you don't have enough can shorten your life.

Creating Balance

16   Diet, exercise, and quitting smoking are important, but they are not the only keys to having a long and healthy life. Meditating might also be important, or planting a garden, or playing cards with friends. If those things calm and relax you, bring you pleasure or make you laugh, then do them.

17   Longevity is a two-sided coin, with quantity on one side and quality on the other. Just as no one wants a great life that's cut short prematurely, no one wants a life that's long but not satisfying. We want to have it both ways—long *and* great. In fact, we can have long, great lives when we balance the five spheres of wellness. ◆

BUILDING ACADEMIC VOCABULARY

The words below are on the Academic Word List.* Find the words in "The Longevity Code." (The number in parentheses is the number of the paragraph.) If you are not sure what a word means, look it up in your dictionary. Then use the words in the sentences that follow.

topic (2, 12)	physical (5)
overall (3)	definitely (6)
overlap (3)	impact (7)
interact (3)	challenge (9)
positive (3)	evidence (12)

1. The dam across the Yangtze River will have a huge _____ on the thousands of people who live in the river valley.

2. He is working as a gardener because he would rather be outside doing _____ work than inside doing mental work.

3. Don't drink citrus juice when you take this medicine. The citric acid in the juice will _____ with the medicine, and the medicine won't work.

4. Both the advertising and marketing departments have a common goal: They want as many people as possible to know about the company's products. As a result, the responsibilities of the two departments _____ somewhat.

5. Because she is taking five difficult classes this semester, getting good grades is a _____.

6. Doctors say that eating a lot of fruit and vegetables has a _____ effect on your health.

7. This evening environmentalists are going to talk about cleaning up our polluted rivers. I'm going to their presentation because I'm interested in the _____.

8. His teacher told him he might get a B as his final grade, or maybe a B+, but _____ not an A.

9. The plane fare was $300, the hotel room was $125 a night, and the food was $200, so the _____ cost of the trip was more than $1,000.

10. Police were quite certain he had committed the crime, but they did not arrest him because they had no _____.

*For an explanation and the complete Academic Word List, see page 157.

DEVELOPING READING SKILLS

◆ UNDERSTANDING THE MAIN IDEAS

Circle the letter of your answer.

According to Dr. Paster, what is the best way to increase your chances of having a long and healthy life?

a. Take care of your body: Cut your cholesterol, lose weight, exercise, stop smoking, and watch your blood pressure. Research shows that taking care of your body has great benefits.

b. Be sure you have health in all five spheres of your life—the physical, mental, family/social, spiritual, and material—because these five spheres overlap and interact.

c. Examine the five spheres of your life—the physical, mental, family/social, spiritual, and material—and decide which sphere is most important to you. Good health in this sphere is critical.

◆ RECOGNIZING SUPPORTING EVIDENCE

 To convince us that they are correct, writers sometimes support their statements with evidence. Being able to recognize supporting evidence can help you become a better reader.

Below are sentences that state Dr. Paster's advice. Match each statement with the scientific evidence that Dr. Paster gives to support it. Write the letter of your answer on the line.

Advice

_____ 1. Be content with what you have.

_____ 2. Have bonds with other people.

_____ 3. Contemplate the meaning and purpose of your life, perhaps by sitting quietly in a garden or by walking in a forest.

_____ 4. Be active, whether you use your muscles to run a marathon or to clean the house.

_____ 5. Try not to become furious over every small frustration.

Evidence

a. Sedentary lifestyles are one of the top ten causes of premature death.

b. Studies indicate that a fit of anger doubles your risk of having a heart attack.

c. A recent study comparing the longevity of three groups of people—couch potatoes, gym rats, and social butterflies—showed that the social butterflies had the longest and healthiest lives.

d. Scientific evidence shows that a spiritual or religious path adds to longevity.

e. Feeling that you don't have enough money can shorten your life.

◆ **APPLYING INFORMATION**

Look at the photos. Are the people in each photo following Dr. Paster's advice for a long, sweet life or not? What makes you think so? Write your answer on a piece of paper.

1.

2.

3.

4.
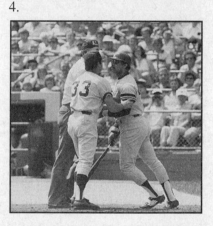

Example:

The women in the first photo appear to be friends, and Dr. Paster says that bonds with other people help us live longer. So, they are following Dr. Paster's advice. But maybe the woman can't buy the dress that she's pointing to because she doesn't have enough money. If not having things makes her ashamed or jealous, it could shorten her life.

READING A CHART

In the chart on page 16, you will find the life-expectancy figures for men and women in ten countries. Look at the chart and discuss the answers to these questions with your classmates.

1. Of the ten countries, where do people have the longest lives?

2. Where do they have the shortest lives?

AVERAGE LIFE EXPECTANCIES IN SELECTED COUNTRIES

	🧍 🧍		
	Average		

CZECH REPUBLIC	71 ＼ 75 ／ 78	CANADA	76 ＼ 80 ／ 83
GREECE	76 ＼ 79 ／ 81	SAUDI ARABIA	67 ＼ 68 ／ 70
NEPAL	58 ＼ 58 ／ 57	TAIWAN	74 ＼ 77 ／ 80
NIGERIA	52 ＼ 52 ／ 52	TURKEY	69 ＼ 72 ／ 74
RUSSIA	62 ＼ 67 ／ 73	UNITED ARAB EMIRATES	72 ＼ 75 ／ 77

Now, turn to page 153, where you will find a chart listing the life-expectancy figures for 25 countries. Use the chart to answer the following questions.

1. Of all 25 countries, where do people live the longest?
2. Where do people have the shortest lives?
3. How do you explain the differences in life-expectancy figures all over the world?
4. Do women live longer than men in every country on the list?

DISCUSSION

A In his book, *The Longevity Code*, Dr. Zorba Paster lists 76 steps you can take to prolong your life. He rates the steps from one star to five stars. The steps with five stars are, in his opinion, very important and will dramatically improve your chances for a longer, sweeter life. The steps with fewer stars are less important. For example, here are three steps from his list and their ratings:

STEPS	STARS
Stay away from tobacco.	★★★★★
Eat breakfast.	★★★
Save money.	★★

1. **Below are 12 steps from Dr. Paster's list. In a small group, guess how many stars Dr. Paster gives each step. Draw one to five stars in the chart.**

STEPS	STARS
1. Don't overdo alcohol.	★★★★
2. Don't use illegal drugs, like heroin or cocaine.	
3. Eat more fruits and vegetables—five to seven per day.	
4. Cut the amount of fat in your diet.	
5. Fasten seat belts.	
6. Take an aspirin every day.	
7. Get enough sleep.	
8. Take care of your teeth and gums.	
9. Have a sense of humor.	
10. Build good relationships with friends.	
11. Own a pet.	
12. Make your workplace fun.	

2. **After you are done guessing, check page 154 to see if you are correct. Then discuss the answers to these questions.**

1. Do you agree with Dr. Paster's ratings?

2. Dr. Paster wrote his book primarily for people who live in the United States. Are there steps on the list that might not be important for people from other countries?

B **Below are some brief descriptions of recent research on longevity. Sit in groups of three. Choose one description to read silently, and summarize it for the other people in your group. Then discuss the answers to the questions below the reading. Explain your answers.**

1. **Eat less, live longer**

U.S. government scientists have learned they can extend the lifespan of rats by cutting the amount of food they eat. In experiments at the National Institutes of Health, scientists gave rats very little food—much less than the rats would eat if nobody were watching—but the food had all the nutrients the rats needed. It's a technique called undernutrition without malnutrition—that is, eating less but eating well. This kind of serious undernutrition dramatically extended the lifespans of the rats: A 30 percent cut in food extended the average lifespan by 30 percent. The technique has not yet been tested in people.

▶ After learning about this research, would you consider eating much less than you do now?

▶ Do you think thin people live longer than heavier people? If you have a story that supports your answer, tell it.

2. **Don't worry, be happy**

Positive emotions may prolong life. A professor at the University of Kentucky studied essays written by a group of women eight decades ago, when they were in their early 20s. He searched the essays for positive emotions, looking for key words such as *happy, joy, love, hopeful,* and *content.* Then, in 2000, he checked to see how long each woman had lived. He discovered that the women who had expressed more positive emotions lived as much as 10 years longer than those expressing fewer positive emotions. The professor believes his study shows that controlling negative feelings is important to leading a longer, healthier life.

▸ Do you think people can actually control how they feel?

▸ Do you think happy people live longer than unhappy people? If you have a story that supports your answer, tell it.

3. **Sweet tooth, long life**

A recent study indicates that people who eat sweets live one year longer than people who don't. Researchers at Harvard University studied the medical records of more than 7,000 men. They discovered that healthy men who ate candy a few times a month added a year to their lives, with some men in the candy-eating group living as long as 95 years. The researchers did not ask the men if the candy they ate was chocolate, but now they wish they had. The researchers suspect that chocolate—not just any kind of candy—extends lifespan. Chocolate is known to have health benefits; perhaps it improves longevity as well as health.

▸ Do you think this research gives people a reason to eat more candy?

▸ After learning about this study, would you consider eating more candy?

WRITING

Choose one of the following topics to write about.

1. Is there a place in your country like Campodimele—a place where people live unusually long and healthy lives? Describe the place.

2. Interview someone who is old and healthy. Ask the person to tell you the secret to his or her health and longevity. Then report what you learned.

3. Who is the oldest person you have ever known? Explain who the person is (or was) and why you think the person has lived (or lived) a long time.

4. Do you agree with Dr. Paster's idea that health in all five spheres is equally important? Or do you think that one sphere is more important than the others? Explain your answer.

5. Have you ever experienced the way the five spheres interact? Write about your experience.

Finding Work That Is Right For You

Have you decided on the work that is right for you? How do you know it's right for you? Below is a list of things people consider when they are thinking about what kind of work they want to do.

Next to each idea on the list, write the first job you think of. (For example, if you wanted to make a lot of money, what work would you do?)

1. making a lot of money   _____
2. helping other people directly   _____
3. doing a job that requires physical strength   _____
4. doing similar tasks each day   _____
5. taking long vacations   _____
6. taking risks as part of my work   _____
7. traveling much of my working time   _____
8. working primarily for myself   _____
9. having job security   _____
10. being creative   _____

Now discuss the answers to these questions with your classmates.

1. Read your answers aloud and listen as your classmates read their answers aloud. Did any of your classmates' answers surprise you? (For example, are there jobs that pay a lot of money in some countries but not in others?)
2. Are there any jobs on your list that you have done or are thinking about doing?
3. Of all the factors above, which one is most important to you in choosing work?

In this unit, you will read about firefighters who survived the World Trade Center collapse and who still believe that they made the right career choice. Next, you will read about a girl who discovered what she loved to do when she was 12 years old. Finally, you will read the advice of a man who believes he knows the secret to finding work that is right for you.

PRE-READING

Look at the photo and read the title of the story on the next page. Then think about these questions. Discuss your answers with your classmates.

▸ Bill Butler, the firefighter in the photo, was inside the World Trade Center when it collapsed on September 11, 2001. He was one of only a few New York City firefighters who came out of the building alive. Could Bill Butler possibly believe that he has "the greatest job in the world"? What do you think?

▸ Tell the class which jobs you think are great. Then listen as your classmates say which jobs they think are great. Write your list of "great jobs" on the board. (You and your classmates do not have to agree on which jobs belong on the list.) Is firefighting on your list of great jobs?

The Greatest Job in the World

1   On September 11, 2001, hundreds of New York City firefighters rushed into the burning World Trade Center. That day, 343 firefighters lost their lives trying to save others. This is the story of six who survived.

2   On the morning of September 11, these six firefighters reported for duty at their firehouse in downtown New York. At 9:46 A.M., they got the call. A plane had just hit the North Tower of the World Trade Center, just a few blocks away. The men arrived at the tower within minutes. As they waited in the lobby for orders from their captain, John Jonas, they heard a rumble and then an explosion. A second plane had hit the South Tower. In the windows of a building across the street, they saw the reflection of the explosion. Firefighter Sal D'Agostino turned to the man next to him. "This is not going to be good," he said.

3   Captain Jonas figured the fire had probably spread down to the 80th floor. He and his men would have to climb 80 flights of stairs with 110 pounds of equipment on their backs. They entered a stairwell and started to walk up.

4   The stairwell was narrow, allowing only two people to pass at a time. On one side of the stairwell, there was a long line of people walking down. On the other side of the stairwell, there was a long line of firefighters walking up. The people descending the stairs encouraged the firefighters. "God bless you, firemen," they said. "Take care . . . Go get 'em . . . Good luck."

5   By the time the firefighters got to the 27th floor, there were no longer any people going down the stairs. Captain Jonas told his men to stop and catch their breath. They still had more than 50 floors to go. Then, while pausing in the stairwell, they heard another rumble—the sound of the South Tower going down. Captain Jonas looked at his men and said, "If that one can go, this one can go. Time to go."

6   The firefighters began their descent. At the 14th floor, they met Josephine, a 60-year-old woman who had walked down from the 73rd floor. She was so tired, she could barely take another step. At the rate she was going, it would take her hours to get out of the building.

7   Captain Jonas told Bill Butler, the strongest man in the group, to help the woman. "Josephine," Bill said, "we're going to get you out of here today."

8   The firefighters were in a race against time. The South Tower had collapsed, and they feared the North Tower might soon follow. Sal D'Agostino remembers looking at the numbers that marked each floor and thinking, "All right, I'm on eight, I'm on seven, I want out of this building now. Let's go." The men encouraged Josephine to move faster. They asked her questions about her family, and they kept telling her, "Josephine, your kids and your grandkids want you home today. We gotta keep moving." Urged on by the firefighters, leaning on Bill Butler, Josephine was moving as fast as she could, but she was exhausted. Her legs were giving out. Tony Falco, one of the firefighters, remembers thinking they had to move faster but adds, "We weren't going to leave her."

9   So Josephine and the firefighters did the best they could, slowly moving down the stairwell. Then they reached the fourth floor. "That's it," Josephine said. "I can't go any more."

10   Captain Jonas remembers feeling "very frustrated. I got all my guys in front of me. We gotta get outta here." He searched the fourth floor for a chair to carry Josephine in.

(continued)

All he could find were swiveling office chairs and some couches, and neither would work.

11   Then there was another rumble. The North Tower was collapsing. Firefighter Matt Komorowski remembers, "The first thing I felt was the incredible rush of air at my back." Then the building started shaking. Sal D'Agostino says, "I got on my side and I crawled to a doorway, and then I just laid there. Waiting for it to come. This is it. This is horrible, and this is it. I said a prayer."

12   When the rumbling finally stopped, it was pitch black, and the firefighters were covered with six inches of dust. But they were alive, scattered now in the stairwell between floors two and four. Bill Butler moved a piece of wall that had fallen near his feet. Under the wall was Josephine. She was alive.

13   Josephine and the firefighters sat in the stairwell, dark as a cave, for several hours. The firefighters remained calm and, for the most part, so did Josephine. Only once she said, "I'm . . . I'm scared." In the calmest voice he could manage, Captain Jonas told her, "Look, we're all a little scared, darlin'. Just hang in there."

14   Then the dust and smoke began to clear, and a shaft of sunlight shone on Josephine and the firefighters. "All of a sudden," Bill Butler says, "everything cleared just for a moment. And I could see that we were at the top of this debris pile. And I thought, 'This is going to be OK. We're going to be OK here.'"

15   One of the firefighters followed the light to a hole, climbed out, and found a rope so that he could lead the others out of the stairwell. But what about Josephine? The firefighters knew that once they left the building, they would have to cross piles of debris. Josephine wouldn't be able to walk across all the rubble, and it would be too dangerous to carry her. So, they waited with Josephine until rescuers came.

16   The rescuers arrived, and an hour later the firefighters and Josephine were out of the ruins of the World Trade Center. The firefighters' determination to stick together—and to stick with Josephine—had saved their lives. When Josephine refused to go any farther than the fourth floor, she kept all seven of them in the only part of the North Tower that remained intact.

17   A week after the collapse of the World Trade Center, reporters interviewed Josephine. She described the six firefighters as "strong, brave, and caring . . . the kindest people I have ever met. When I was scared, they held my hand. They took off their jackets and gave them to me when I was cold. They told me not to be afraid, they would get me out. And they did." She added that when they were trapped in the stairwell, she thought the building was going to start moving again. One of the firefighters told her that if the building started to move again, they would put her in a doorway. And he would cover her body with his.

18   Reporters asked the firefighters if they had any thoughts about leaving the job. All six men said they would not. Sal D'Agostino said, "I think everybody thinks about it. But I'm not going. I've got to be true to me." Matt Komorowski explained, "I think being a fireman runs through your core. And even if bad things are happening all around that core, you always have that core." Tony Falco added, "I don't think I'm going to leave. It's the greatest job in the world." ◆

GETTING THE BIG PICTURE

Circle the letter of your answer.

What is the main reason the six firefighters in the story survived?

a. The men had 110 pounds of equipment on their backs. Their equipment made it possible for them to breathe even though the air was filled with dust and smoke.

b. The fire spread down to the 80th floor and stopped there. The firefighters did not go higher than the 27th floor.

c. They refused to leave one another, and they refused to leave Josephine. She kept them in the only part of the building that remained intact.

BUILDING VOCABULARY

◆ RECALLING NEW WORDS

The words below are from the story. Write the correct word or words on the line.

urged	figured	exhausted	frustrated
debris	trapped	scattered	pitch black
intact	collapse	reflection	reported for duty

1. The six firefighters came to work every day at 9:00 A.M., so they had just _____ when the first plane hit the World Trade Center.

2. The windows of the building across the street were like a mirror. The firefighters could see the _____ of the explosion in the glass.

3. Captain Jonas knew where the plane had hit the North Tower, and he knew how fast a fire spreads. He _____ it had probably spread to the 80th floor.

4. The South Tower had fallen down, and the firefighters were afraid the North Tower would _____, too.

5. When the firefighters met Josephine, she had already walked down 59 flights of stairs. She was _____.

6. "Keep moving," the firefighters told Josephine. They _____ her to move faster.

7. Captain Jonas was in a dangerous situation, and there was nothing he could do about it. Josephine would not go any farther, and he could not find a chair to carry her in. He felt _____.

8. After the North Tower collapsed, the firefighters could see nothing because of the smoke and dust. It was _____.

9. The firefighters could not get out of the building. They were _____ in the stairwell.

10. Some firefighters were on the second floor, some were on the third floor, and some were on the fourth floor. They were _____ between floors two and four.

11. The World Trade Center was destroyed. Where the building once stood, there was now only a pile of _____.

12. The only part of the World Trade Center that was still standing was the stairwell between the second and fourth floors. Josephine had kept them all in the only part of the building that was _____.

◆ **UNDERSTANDING SPECIAL EXPRESSIONS**

Complete the sentences to show that you understand the meanings of the new words. There may be several correct ways to complete each sentence.

1. *once** = **immediately after something happens**

   Example: Once you've taken the medicine, <u>you'll feel better</u>.

   a. The firefighters knew that once they left the building, they would have to

   _____.

   b. Once he's saved enough money, he can _____.

   c. Once they've finished their homework, they can _____.

2. *could barely* = **almost could not**

   Example: The theater was so dark we could barely <u>find our way to our seats</u>.

   a. Josephine was so tired she could barely _____.

   b. He spoke so softly we could barely _____.

   c. Her handwriting was so bad I could barely _____.

DEVELOPING READING SKILLS

◆ **UNDERSTANDING CHRONOLOGICAL ORDER**

Read each group of four sentences. One of the sentences is not in chronological order. Draw a line through the sentence that is not in the correct place.

1. The six firefighters arrive at the North Tower of the World Trade Center.
   They enter a stairwell and start walking up.
   ~~They feel an incredible rush of wind at their backs.~~
   They stop to catch their breath at the 27th floor.

2. The South Tower collapses, and Captain Jonas orders his men out of the building.
   The firefighters begin descending the stairs.
   They meet Josephine and tell her they will help her get out of the building.
   People who are descending the stairs encourage the firefighters.

*The word *once* usually means "one time," but it can also mean "immediately after something happens."

3. At the fourth floor, Josephine says she can go no farther.
   She tells the firefighters she is scared.
   Captain Jonas searches for a chair to carry Josephine.
   The North Tower collapses.

4. The firefighters are trapped in the stairwell between floors two and four.
   Bill Butler finds Josephine under a wall.
   The firefighters ask Josephine questions about her family.
   The smoke and dust clear.

5. One of the firefighters climbs out of the building through a hole, finds a rope, and returns.
   The firefighters decide not to carry Josephine across the piles of rubble.
   They encourage her to move faster.
   Rescuers arrive, and the firefighters leave the building with Josephine.

◆ UNDERSTANDING CAUSE AND EFFECT

Complete the sentences with information from the story. Write your answer on the line. There may be several correct ways to complete each sentence.

1. The firefighters arrived at the World Trade Center only minutes after a plane hit it because *their firehouse was only a few blocks away.*

2. Only two people could walk side by side in the stairwell because _____
   _____.

3. Captain Jonas chose Bill Butler to help Josephine because _____
   _____.

4. Josephine was exhausted because _____
   _____.

5. Firefighter Tony Falco says he will not leave his job because _____
   _____.

◆ SUMMARIZING

 Summarizing is a good way to check your comprehension. When you write a summary, you include only the main information and not the details. A summary is shorter than the original reading.

Imagine that a reporter asks Bill Butler to summarize what happened on September 11, 2001. Bill Butler tells the story below. Complete his story on a separate piece of paper. Include only the main information and not the details.

"Our firehouse is just a few blocks from the World Trade Center, so we got there minutes after the first plane hit the North Tower. Our captain told us the fire had probably spread to the 80th floor. We entered a stairwell and started walking up . . ."

The theme of this unit is "finding work that is right for you." Clearly, the firefighters in the first story found work that is right for them. So did Ruth Reichl, the writer of the next story. Although she probably didn't realize it at the time, Ms. Reichl discovered her future profession when she was only 12 years old.

When Ruth was 12, she left her home in New York City to attend a school in Montreal, Canada. Montreal is in the French-speaking part of Canada, and Ruth went to school there to learn French. One weekend, a Canadian classmate named Beatrice du Croix invited Ruth to her home. Beatrice, Ruth found out, was from a very wealthy family. In the following story, Ruth describes her first lunch with Beatrice's family.

As you read this description of Ruth's lunch with the du Croix family, try to guess which profession Ruth chose when she became an adult. When you're finished reading the excerpt from *Tender at the Bone*, turn to page 154 to see which two professions Ruth actually chose.

From *Tender at the Bone* by Ruth Reichl

Monsieur[1] du Croix sat at the head of the long table. "Papa!" said Beatrice happily. He got up to kiss her and I saw how short he was. Still, with his snowy white hair and sapphire blue eyes he was an imposing figure.

"*Asseyez-vous*,"[2] he commanded, picking up a ladle by his plate and dipping it into a tureen of soup. A butler stood before him holding out a bowl, and he slowly filled it with a thick orange liquid. Then the butler walked solemnly around the table, distributing the bowls. The soup was fragrant and steamed invitingly. I sat, tantalized, waiting for Madame[3] du Croix to lift her spoon.

Finally she did. I dipped my own spoon into the thick liquid and brought it to my mouth. With the first sip I knew that I had never really eaten before. The initial taste was pure carrot, followed by cream, butter, a bit of nutmeg. Then I swallowed and my whole mouth and throat filled with the echo of rich chicken stock. I took another sip and it began all over again. I ate as if in a dream.

The butler set a roast before Beatrice's father, while the maid removed our empty bowls. Slowly the roast was carved and then the butler moved majestically around the table serving the meat.

It was just a filet of beef. But I had never tasted anything like this sauce, a mixture of red wine, butter, herbs, and mushrooms. It was like autumn distilled in a spoon. A shiver went down my back. "This sauce!" I exclaimed involuntarily. The sound echoed through the polite conversation at the table and I put my hand to my mouth. Monsieur du Croix laughed.

(continued)

[1]**Monsieur** = Mr.
[2]**Asseyez-vous** = Sit down.
[3]**Madame** = Mrs.

"Your friend likes to eat," he said to Beatrice. He seemed pleased. He held up one of the *pommes soufflés*[4] that the butler had set on his plate and said, "You will like these, I think." He told the butler to serve me immediately.

"Taste!" he commanded. I put the puff of potato in my mouth; it was a magic potato chip, a crisp mouthful of hot air, salt, and flavor. Monsieur smiled again. "Incredible, no?"

"Incredible, yes!" I said.

Monsieur du Croix turned to his wife. "This child likes to eat!" he said for the second time. He winked at me. "You will like the dessert, I think," he said. "A whole wheel of Brie[5] has just arrived from France. Have you ever tasted a real French Brie?"

I had not. He cut me a large wedge and set it on a plate. He surrounded it with a few grapes ("From Sicily," he murmured, almost to himself, "not those sad, sour Canadian fruits") and told the butler to bring it to me. "Eat it with your fork," Monsieur commanded, "It would be wasted on bread."

I cut a piece, carefully removing the rind the way I had always seen it done. "No, no, no," said Monsieur du Croix angrily. I jumped. "Eat the skin," he said. "It is part of the experience. Do you think the cheesemaker aged this ten weeks just to have you throw away half of his effort?"

"*Bien sûr*,"[6] I said meekly, putting the rind into my mouth. I felt Monsieur du Croix watching as I ate the strong, slippery cheese. It was so powerful I felt the tips of my ears go pink. The hairs on the back of my neck stood up. I closed my eyes. When I opened them Monsieur du Croix was watching me the way a teacher watches a particularly apt pupil. ◆

[4]*pommes soufflés* = a baked food that has a lot of air and is made with potatoes, eggs, flour, and milk
[5]**Brie** = a soft cheese

[6]*Bien sûr* = Of course.

◆ **SHARING YOUR TRUE STORIES**

Discuss the answers to these questions with your classmates.

1. Ruth describes the Brie cheese as "strong," "slippery," and "powerful." When she ate it, the tips of her ears went pink and the hairs on the back of her neck stood up. With your classmates, find the words Ruth uses to describe the soup, the filet of beef, and the *pommes soufflés*. Now imagine that someone from another country is coming to dinner at your home. What would you give your guest to eat? Think about a favorite meal that is typical of the food of your native country. Then describe it to a partner from a different country. Try to use words that will help your partner imagine how the food looks and tastes.

2. Have you chosen the work you want to do? When you look back on your childhood, can you see now that you already had an interest in that kind of work then? (For example: You were a child who loved computers, and now you're studying computer science.)

In this unit, you have read about people who found work that is right for them. First, you read about the New York City firefighters, who believe that firefighting "runs through your core." Next, you read about Ruth Reichl, the child who liked to eat. She became the editor of a magazine about food and the restaurant critic for the *New York Times*—a job that required her to eat at New York City restaurants and write about the food.

Neither of these stories would surprise Parker Palmer. Dr. Palmer is a teacher and writer who believes he knows how people can find work that will bring them joy. According to Dr. Palmer, the way to find work that is right for you is to become "the person you have always been."

Before you read, think about what Dr. Palmer means by "becoming the person you have always been."

Becoming Yourself

1   Every time Parker Palmer's little granddaughter comes to visit, he observes her. He notices what she likes and doesn't like. He notices how she moves, what she does, and what she says. Then he writes his observations down. When his granddaughter is older, he will put his observations in a letter and give the letter to her. His letter will begin something like this: "Here is a sketch of who you were from your earliest days in the world. It is not a complete picture— only you can draw that. But it was sketched by a person who loves you very much. Perhaps these notes will help you do what I finally did in my own life: Remember who you were when you first arrived and reclaim the gift of true self."

A future restaurant critic?

2   Dr. Palmer will give his granddaughter the letter when she is in her late teens or early 20s, when she will probably be deciding what kind of work she wants to do. Dr. Palmer hopes that if his granddaughter knows her "true self," she will choose work that is right for her.

3   Young people who are trying to decide on a career often ask themselves, "What should I do with my life?" Dr. Palmer thinks it is more useful to ask, "Who am I? What is my nature?" He points out that everything in the universe has a nature, which has its limits as well as its potentials. This is a truth that people who work daily with natural materials know. A potter, for example, cannot simply tell the clay what to do. The clay presses back on the potter's hands, telling her what it can and cannot do. If she fails to listen to the clay, her pottery will be frail and unattractive. An engineer cannot tell his materials what they must do. He must understand the nature of the steel or the wood or the stone he is working with. If he does not,

(continued)

the bridge or building he designs could collapse. Human beings, Dr. Palmer says, also have a nature, with limits as well as potentials. When choosing a career, we must understand the material we are working with, just as the potter understands the clay and the engineer the steel. To find work that is right for us, we must know our nature. Attempts to override that nature always fail.

4   It is not always easy for us to know exactly what our nature is. Sometimes we are discouraged from following our natural inclinations, and we lose track of what they are. When we are young, we are surrounded by expectations—the expectations of our families, our teachers, and, later, our employers. Often these people are not trying to understand our nature; instead, they are trying to fit us into slots. Sometimes racism, sexism, or tradition determines the slots people choose for us. For example, a little girl who wants to be a carpenter when she grows up is told that girls cannot be carpenters, but she could be a teacher. Or an oldest son who wants to be an artist is persuaded to take over the family business instead of studying art. We feel the pressure of others' expectations, and we betray our nature in order to be accepted.

5   Dr. Palmer maintains that if we lose track of our true self, it is possible to pick up the trail again. One way is to look for clues from our younger years, when we lived closer to our nature. That is how he found his way back to his true self. In his book *Let Your Life Speak,* he writes:

6   In grade school, I became fascinated with the mysteries of flight. As many boys did in those days, I spent endless hours, after school and on weekends, designing, making, flying, and (usually) crashing model airplanes made of fragile wood.

Unlike most boys, however, I also spent long hours creating eight- and twelve-page books about aviation. I would turn a sheet of paper sideways; draw a vertical line down the middle; make diagrams of, say, the cross-section of a wing; roll the sheet into a typewriter; and type a caption explaining how air moving across the wing creates a vacuum that lifts the plane. Then I would fold that sheet in half along with several others I had made, staple the collection together down the spine, and painstakingly illustrate the cover.

I had always thought that the meaning of this paperwork was obvious: fascinated with flight, I wanted to be a pilot, or perhaps an aeronautical engineer. But recently, when I found a couple of these books in a cardboard box, I suddenly saw the truth, and it was more obvious than I had imagined. I didn't want to be a pilot or anything related to aviation. I wanted to be an author, to make books—a task I have been attempting from the third grade to this very moment!

9   When he found the books he had made as a boy, Parker Palmer realized that for most of his adult life he had not been following his natural inclinations. He says that he tried to ignore his nature, hide from it, and run from it, and he thinks he is not alone. He believes that there is a universal tendency to want to be someone else—but that it is more important to be oneself.

10   And so, Dr. Palmer observes his granddaughter. He hopes that someday his observations will help her remember what she was like when she was very young. He hopes that she will become the person she was born to be and find work that will bring her joy. He hopes, in short, that she will grow up to be the person she has always been. ◆

BUILDING VOCABULARY

◆ IDENTIFYING THE CORRECT DEFINITION

The words in italics have several meanings. What do they mean in the sentences below? Circle the letter of your answer. (The definitions are adapted from the *Longman Advanced American Dictionary.***)**

1. It is not always easy for us to know exactly what our *nature* is.
   a. everything in the physical world that is not controlled by humans, such as wild plants and animals, earth and rocks, and the weather: *I've always been a nature lover.*
   b. the qualities which make someone different from others: *It's her nature to be generous.*

2. Parker Palmer's letter to his granddaughter will begin, "Here is a *sketch* of who you were from your earliest days in the world."
   a. a simple, quickly made drawing that does not show much detail: *Renoir's sketches for his paintings*
   b. a short written or spoken description: *The speaker gave us a sketch of life in the 1890s.*

3. We feel the *pressure* of others' expectations.
   a. an attempt to persuade someone by using influence, arguments, or threats: *So far, she has resisted pressure to tell her story to the newspapers.*
   b. a way of working or living that causes you a lot of anxiety, especially because you feel you have too many things to do: *I just can't take the pressure at work anymore.*
   c. the force or weight that is being put on something: *To stop the bleeding, put pressure directly on the wound.*
   d. the weight of the air: *Low pressure often brings rain.*

4. We *betray* our nature in order to be accepted.
   a. to be disloyal to someone who trusts you, so that they are hurt or upset: *She betrayed her friend when she told everyone his secret.*
   b. to be disloyal to your country, for example by giving secret information to its enemies: *He betrayed his country for money.*
   c. to stop supporting your beliefs and principles, especially in order to get power or avoid trouble: *He said he would never lie to anyone, but he betrayed his principles when he told his teacher that no one had helped him write his essay.*
   d. to show feelings that you are trying to hide: *His face betrayed his disappointment at not getting the job.*

5. Dr. Palmer *maintains* that if we lose track of our true self, it is possible to pick up the trail again.
   a. to make something continue in the same way as before: *They hope to maintain peace in the region.*
   b. to take care of something so that it stays in good condition: *They maintain all the equipment in the office.*
   c. to strongly express your belief that something is true: *For centuries people maintained that the world was flat.*

6. "I would staple the collection of papers together down the *spine*."
   a. the row of bones down the center of the back of humans and some animals: *The human spine is made up of 33 separate bones.*
   b. the side of a book where the pages are fastened together: *What you see on a library shelf is a book's spine.*
   c. a stiff, sharp-pointed part of an animal or plant: *Touching a cactus spine can be a painful experience!*

DEVELOPING READING SKILLS

◆ UNDERSTANDING THE MAIN IDEAS

Circle the letter of the best answer.

1. Parker Palmer believes that to find work that is right for us, we must
   a. know our nature.
   b. meet our families' expectations.
   c. work with natural materials.

2. According to Dr. Palmer, it is sometimes difficult for us to know our nature because
   a. our parents and grandparents do not take the time to observe us and tell us what our nature is.
   b. our families, teachers, and employers discourage us from following our natural inclinations, and we no longer remember what our nature is.
   c. human beings, unlike natural materials, do not always have a nature.

3. Imagine that a 21-year-old man tells Dr. Palmer that he doesn't know exactly what his nature is. What would Dr. Palmer tell him to do?
   a. "Ask your family and teachers, 'What should I do with my life?'"
   b. "Don't try to discover your nature; attempts to discover it always fail."
   c. "Look for clues in your childhood; try to remember what you liked and didn't like when you were young."

4. When Parker Palmer found his old books in a cardboard box, he realized that
    a. he should have become a pilot or an aeronautical engineer.
    b. he did not use his free time wisely when he was a boy.
    c. he had not followed his natural inclinations for most of his adult life.

5. Why is Parker Palmer observing his granddaughter and writing down his observations?
    a. He is a writer, and he will include his observations in a book about finding the right work.
    b. He believes his observations will help her choose the right work when she is older.
    c. He believes that he might not be alive when she is an adult and wants her to remember their time together.

◆ EVALUATING STATEMENTS

Below are some statements which reflect Parker Palmer's opinions.

Read each statement. Check (✓) *Agree* or *Disagree.* Then compare your answers with a partner's. Explain to your partner why you agree or disagree. If you have had an experience that supports your opinion, tell your partner about it.

1. To find work that is right for us, we must know our nature.   ❑ Agree   ❑ Disagree

2. It is not always easy for us to know what our nature is.   ❑ Agree   ❑ Disagree

3. We sometimes feel the pressure of others' expectations, and we betray our nature in order to be accepted.   ❑ Agree   ❑ Disagree

4. If we lose track of our "true self," one way to pick up the trail is to look for clues in our younger years.   ❑ Agree   ❑ Disagree

◆ APPLYING INFORMATION

The boy in the picture on the next page is three years old. He is handing his father a tool so that his father can fix a truck. The boy's father says his son has been helping him fix cars and trucks ever since he could walk.

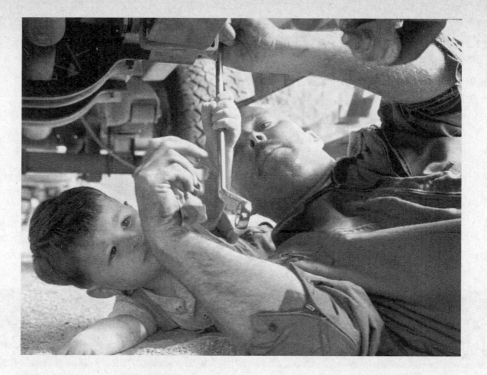

Discuss the answers to these questions with your classmates, or write your answers on a separate piece of paper.

1. Would Parker Palmer say that the boy should be a mechanic when he grows up?

2. Do you think the boy should be a mechanic when he grows up?

READING A CHART

On page 34 is a list of the 15 best jobs in the United States for the 21st century. These jobs are considered best for three reasons:

▶ The salaries are high.

▶ There are a large number of job openings.

▶ The jobs are in fields that are expected to grow.

1. Before you and your classmates read the list, try to guess which jobs are on it. Write your guesses on the board. Then read this information about U.S. society:

▶ After World War II, there was a big rise (a "boom") in the U.S. birth rate. Americans born during the years following the war, from 1946 to 1964, are called "baby boomers." They make up 31 percent of the U.S. population. Most "baby boomers" are now over 50 years old.

▶ Over half of all families in the U.S. have computers in their homes.

▶ Half of all Americans have money invested in the stock market.

▶ Every year, 17.3 million lawsuits are filed in the United States.

2. Does having the information about U.S. society make it easier to predict which jobs might be on the "best jobs" list? Are there any jobs you want to add to your list? Now read the list below to see how many of your guesses were right.

TOP 15 JOBS FOR THE 21ST CENTURY			
JOB[1]	AVERAGE SALARY	ANNUAL JOB OPENINGS	PERCENT OF GROWTH
1. Most jobs in computer science	$ 52,675	524,397	82%
2. Stock broker, financial adviser	$ 48,090	61,084	41%
3. Advertising, marketing, public relations, sales manager	$ 57,300	89,237	23%
4. General manager, top executive	$ 55,890	421,006	16%
5. University professor	$ 46,600	139,101	23%
6. Medical services manager[2]	$ 48,870	31,238	33%
7. Electrical engineer	$ 62,260	29,636	26%
8. Nurse	$ 40,690	195,231	22%
9. Physician	$102,020	32,563	21%
10. Management analyst[3]	$ 49,470	23,831	28%
11. Secondary school teacher	$ 37,890	133,585	23%
12. Police officer	$ 37,710	51,739	32%
13. Lawyer	$ 78,170	38,182	17%
14. Special education teacher	$ 37,850	36,540	34%
15. Legal assistant	$ 32,760	33,971	62%

[1] Rankings are based on the combined factors of salary, job openings, and rate of growth.
[2] A medical services manager might be the director of a hospital or nursing home.
[3] A management analyst examines a business to be sure work is done in the most efficient way. For example, a management analyst might examine the way a business keeps track of inventory or the way people in the business communicate with one another.

3. Discuss the answers to these questions with your classmates.

1. These top jobs are in the United States. Are there any jobs on the list that would not be top jobs in your native country? Cross them out. Then compare your list with that of a classmate from another country.

2. How do these salaries compare with salaries for the same work in your native country?

3. If you discovered that the work you want to do is not on a list like the one above, would you consider choosing different work? Why or why not?

4. What do you think about the three reasons (salary, number of openings, future growth) for putting a job on this list? Are there other reasons which should have been considered, too?

5. What do you think Parker Palmer would think of this list?

DISCUSSION

Parker Palmer believes that you must know your nature if you want to find work that is right for you. One way to discover what he calls your "true self" is to look for clues in your younger years. He gives himself as an example: He was a boy who made books in his free time; that was a clue that he should be an author.

1. Find five ways to complete the sentence, "I was a kid who . . ."

Example: I was a kid who

▶ *was very shy.* _____

▶ *was neat and tidy.* _____

▶ *was diligent.* _____

▶ *hated sports.* _____

▶ *liked taking things apart to see how they worked.* _____

Now complete the sentence. Write your answers on the lines.

I was a kid who:

▶ _____

▶ _____

▶ _____

▶ _____

▶ _____

2. Read your description of yourself as a child to a small group of classmates. Then tell your classmates what kind of work you want to do (or already do). Do you and your classmates see clues in your description that you have chosen work that is right for you? What are the clues?

WRITING

Choose one of the following topics to write about.

1. What kind of work do you plan to do? (Or, what kind of work do you do?) Explain why you chose that work.

2. Have you ever had an experience like Ruth Reichl's? Can you look back on a childhood experience and see that the right work for you was already clear then? Describe your experience.

3. Ask someone who knew you when you were a child to describe what you were like when you were very young. Ask the person to describe anything special that you said or did. Write their memories of you.

4. Can you think of people in your own life who, like Ruth Reichl and the firefighters, have found work they love? Describe one of those people and the work he or she does.

5. Interview someone about his or her work. First, make a list of possible questions you could ask, for example:

   ▶ What do you do on a typical workday?

   ▶ What do you like about your work?

   ▶ What don't you like about your work?

   ▶ Why did you choose this work?

Tape record your interview or take notes. At home, listen to the recording or review your notes. Then decide what information you would like to include in a short essay about the person you interviewed. (You might want to focus on the answer to only one of your questions.)

Geeks

The theme of this unit is "geeks." Geek is a slang term—it is new, informal language. Geeks are people who are not popular because they wear clothes that are not fashionable or because they behave strangely. But the author of a book titled Geeks writes that a geek is simply "someone who is passionate about technology and has a talent for working with computers."

1. Talk about the sentences below. Can you guess what they mean? Write an explanation for each sentence. Then look on page 154 to see if you guessed correctly.

    ▶ "My computer crashed." _____
    _____

    ▶ "I work for an Internet start-up company." _____
    _____

    ▶ "I'm online for a couple of hours every evening, surfing the Net." _____
    _____

2. In a small group, make a list of computer-related terms you might expect to find in this unit. Choose one or two terms to share with the class and briefly explain what the words mean.

In this unit, you will read the story of two young men whose talent for working with computers brought them phenomenal success. Next, you will read the story of a woman who started her own computer company. Finally, you will learn what geeks are and what they are not. (Perhaps you will discover that you or someone you know is a geek!)

PRE-READING

The young men in the photo had a talent for working with computers, and that talent brought them phenomenal success. Look at the photo and read the title of the story on the next page. With your classmates, make a list of questions you think the story will answer.

Example:

▶ *How old are they?*

▶ *Are they friends?*

When you have finished reading the story, look back at the questions you and your classmates wrote. Which questions did the story answer?

Two Yahoos

1   Imagine a Hollywood movie with this plot: Lily Yang, a young widow, leaves Taiwan and immigrates to the United States, with her ten-year old son, Chih-Yuan. After the family settles in California, Chih-Yuan changes his first name to Jerry and heads off to school, knowing only one word of English, the word *shoe.* Jerry learns English quickly; he is exceptionally bright and becomes a straight-A student. When he graduates from high school, he wins a scholarship to a top university, where he becomes friends with David Filo, a fellow student. Together Jerry and David start an Internet company that makes them both billionaires within five years.

2   If you think this could happen only in a Hollywood movie, you are wrong. It could happen in California's Silicon Valley.[1] And it did.

3   In 1993, Jerry Yang and David Filo were studying for their doctorates in electrical engineering at Stanford University in California. They did their work side by side at desks that the university provided for them. But when they sat down at their computers, they often found themselves "surfing the Web"—looking for interesting sites on the Internet, which was new then—instead of working, like two kids watching TV rather than doing their homework.

4   Jerry and David thought the Internet was fascinating and at the same time frustrating. They were constantly asking each other, "Hey— where was that cool page we saw the other day?" Sometimes it would take them hours to find a Web site again. The problem was this: The only way to get to an Internet site was to type in its exact address (called its *url,* for "universal resource locator"). A url could be a long string of numbers and letters like this: *http://www.wnn.or.jp/wnn-t/index_e.html.* If the address was not perfectly right—if one letter was left out or one dot was misplaced—it was impossible to get to that Web site. Imagine a library with no card catalog. The only way to find a book would be to know exactly where it was. That was the state of the Internet in 1993.

5   David developed software so that Jerry could compile a list of their favorite Web sites; that way, they could revisit them whenever they wanted to. Jerry kept adding sites to the list, and it quickly got so long that it needed to be organized. Jerry thought back to a part-time job he'd had shelving books in the university library. He remembered how the books were organized into categories and subcategories, and he decided to organize his list of Web sites in the same way. "Sports," for example, became one category, with subcategories like "sumo wrestling" and "basketball."

6   Jerry called the list "Jerry's Guide to the World Wide Web" and posted it on the Internet in the spring of 1994. Friends told friends about "Jerry's Guide," and the number of people viewing it doubled every month—from hundreds, to thousands, to hundreds of thousands. Telephone calls and e-mail suggesting sites to add were coming in faster than Jerry and David could handle them. Jerry and David abandoned their studies altogether and started working 20 hours a day on Jerry's list, often sleeping on the floor next to their computers. Their hobby had become an obsession.

7   Late one night, Jerry and David began talking about changing the name of the Web site. "Jerry's Guide to the World Wide Web" no longer seemed appropriate, as David was working on the site as much as Jerry. They flipped through a dictionary, looking for

[1] **Silicon Valley** = an area of California between San Francisco and San Jose that is a center of the computer industry.

(continued)

possible new names, and came across the word *yahoo*. The dictionary gave two definitions of the word: "a rough or noisy person" and "a word shouted when you find something you're excited about." They liked the word—they thought it reflected the Wild West nature of the Internet. Just for fun, they added an exclamation point. Yahoo!, they thought, was a name people would remember. Indeed it was.

8   By the end of 1994, the Yahoo! Web site was getting one million hits a day, and Stanford's computer system was crashing under the strain. University officials told Jerry and David they would have to move their hobby off campus. When word got out that Yahoo! was looking for a new home, Jerry and David got job offers from several giant telecommunications companies. The offer they finally accepted, however, was not a job offer, but an offer of money. A venture capitalist gave Jerry and David $1 million to start their own business. In exchange, he took a 25 percent stake in Yahoo! Yahoo!, the corporation, was born.

9   When Yahoo! officially opened for business, its corporate offices were typical for an Internet start-up company. Newspaper accounts from 1995 give this description:

> All the office furniture is purple and yellow, the official corporate colors. In purple-painted cubicles, 16 employees, called "surfers," sit in front of computers and review Web site submissions, rejecting some and deciding where to put the ones they accept. All of the surfers are in their early 20s, wear T-shirts, and park their bicycles next to their desks. From time to time, David Filo, barefoot and wearing torn jeans, emerges from his office, which is cluttered with old newspapers, CDs, a pair of purple roller blades, and crumpled Coke cans. Often David doesn't leave Yahoo! headquarters for days—he sleeps under his desk—and when he does leave, he drives away in a dilapidated 1981 Datsun, its tailpipe dragging on the ground. To top it off,

Jerry and David carry business cards that identify their positions in the company as the "Chief Yahoos."

10   But the Chief Yahoos knew what they were doing. Their competitors were in a race to develop powerful technology to collect as many Internet sites as possible for their directories. Some even used robot computers, called "spiders," that searched the Internet day and night, looking for new sites. Yahoo! thought its competitors were on the wrong track. Jerry and David suspected that people didn't necessarily want access to every site on the Internet; they needed help sorting through all the sites that were out there. That is what Yahoo! would do. Instead of buying robot computers, Yahoo! hired more people. People, not software programs, would choose Web sites for the Yahoo! directory and put them in the appropriate categories. The final work would always be done by humans.

11   Jerry and David's instincts were right. Yahoo! became the most popular site on the World Wide Web, attracting 100 million people a month. These were the huge numbers advertisers wanted, and corporations started paying millions for advertising spots on the Yahoo! site. Yahoo! was a gold mine, and Jerry and David had struck it rich.

12   In the past few years, Yahoo!'s fortunes have been up and down, but Jerry Yang and David Filo don't seem to care much whether they personally make or lose money. All that matters is Yahoo! itself. Even after Yahoo! made them millionaires, their lives didn't change much: David still drove his old Datsun, and Jerry still dressed like a student, wearing Levi jeans and a green plastic Yahoo! watch. They still worked long hours, too. Jerry told a newspaper reporter, "Yahoo! is such a big part of my life that I don't think of this as a job." Yahoo! has become a billion-dollar corporation, but to David and Jerry it will always be what it was in 1993—a hobby and an obsession. ◆

GETTING THE BIG PICTURE

What are the reasons for Jerry and David's phenomenal success with Yahoo!?
Check (✓) three reasons.

❑ Jerry and David were bright and had a talent for working with computers.

❑ They had doctorates in computer science and years of experience working with computers.

❑ They worked hard—sometimes 20 hours a day.

❑ They got help from giant telecommunications companies.

❑ They were among the first to develop a way to organize sites on the Internet and help people find Web sites.

BUILDING VOCABULARY

◆ RECALLING NEW WORDS

Match the words below with those in italics. Write your answer on the line.

cubicles	stake in	headquarters	on the wrong track
state	gold mine	a fellow student	venture capitalist
settle		flipping through	

_____ 1. After they entered the United States, the Yang family decided to *make their home* in California.

_____ 2. David Filo was *someone who studied with Jerry* at Stanford University.

_____ 3. In 1993, the only way to find an Internet site was to know its exact address. That was the *condition* of the Internet then.

_____ 4. Jerry and David were *quickly turning the pages* of the dictionary, searching for a name for their Web site.

_____ 5. Jerry and David got $1 million from a *person who lends money to people who want to start their own business.*

_____ 6. The man gave Jerry and David $1 million, and they gave him a 25 percent *share of* Yahoo!.

_____ 7. Yahoo!'s employees worked in *small, partly enclosed spaces in a large office.*

_____ 8. Often David didn't leave Yahoo!'s *main office* for days.

_____ 9. Jerry and David thought their competitors were *doing things that made it unlikely they would succeed.*

_____ 10. Yahoo! had become a *business that produced large profits,* and Jerry and David had struck it rich.

◆ UNDERSTANDING SPECIAL EXPRESSIONS

Complete the sentences to show that you understand the meanings of the new words. There may be several correct ways to complete each sentence.

1. *to come across* = to discover by chance

Example: While looking through a pile of CDs that were on sale, I came across *one that I'd been wanting to buy for a long time*   .

    a. Jerry and David were flipping though a dictionary, looking for a new name for their Web site, when they came across _____
_____.

    b. While looking though an old photo album, he came across _____
_____.

    c. While cleaning my closet, I came across _____
_____.

2. *word got out* = many people heard

Example: When word got out that the new nuclear power plant would be only one mile from the town, *environmental groups protested*   .

    a. When word got out that Yahoo! was looking for a new home, Jerry and David _____
_____.

    b. When word got out that the new store would give free TVs to its first 100 customers, _____
_____.

    c. When word got out that the professor had given a failing grade to everyone in the class, _____
_____.

3. *to top it off* = in addition to all the other bad things that happened

Example: When I took a shower, there was no hot water. To top it off, *the*   *shampoo bottle was empty*   .

    a. At first, Yahoo! didn't seem like a serious company: The office was purple and yellow, the employees wore T-shirts, and David Filo walked around barefoot. To top it off, _____
_____.

    b. On the day of the picnic, it rained and the weather turned cold. To top it off, _____
_____.

    c. On the day of the exam, I overslept and then missed the bus. To top it off, _____
_____.

DEVELOPING READING SKILLS

◆ **UNDERSTANDING THE MAIN IDEAS**

Imagine that you are Jerry Yang, and a reporter asks you the questions below. Write your answers to the reporter's questions on a separate piece of paper. The first one is done for you.

1. You once said that you and David found the Internet "frustrating" in its early days. Why was it frustrating? *To get to an Internet site, you had to know its exact address. Sometimes David and I would find a really cool Web page, and then a few days later we couldn't find it again.*

2. I understand that Yahoo! began as a list of Web sites that you organized. How did you organize them?

3. When Yahoo! opened for business in 1995, its corporate offices were described as "typical for an Internet start-up." What did the offices look like?

4. How was Yahoo! different from its competitors?

5. How has becoming a multimillionaire changed your life?

◆ **SCANNING FOR INFORMATION**

 Scanning is reading quickly to find specific information. If, for example, you wanted the answer to the question "Which university did Jerry and David attend?" you could scan the story for the information. You would move your eyes quickly across the pages, perhaps looking for words that begin with a capital letter, until you found "Stanford"—the information you wanted.

Scan the story for the words below. Think of questions that would give you these answers. Write your questions on the lines.

Question	Answer
1. *What is Jerry's Chinese name?*	Chih-Yuan
2. _____	"sumo wrestling" and "basketball"
3. _____	in the spring of 1994
4. _____	"a rough or noisy person"
5. _____	purple and yellow
6. _____	a 1981 Datsun
7. _____	"spiders"

◆ MAKING INFERENCES

 To *infer* is to use information you have to make a logical guess. For example, let's say Jerry Yang is being interviewed on TV. He says, "When we came here, she didn't know how she would earn a living. She was very brave." You know from the story that Jerry and his mother came from Taiwan, so you can infer that he is talking about his mother. You cannot be sure he is talking about her, but it would be a logical guess.

Jerry Yang made the following statements to reporters in interviews. (The statements are not in the story.) Use the information you know from the story to infer what he is talking about. Write your answer on the line.

1. "**It** started because David got sick of me asking him where everything was."
   What is "it"? *"Jerry's Guide to the World Wide Web," which later became Yahoo!*

2. "A lot of people found **it** easy to remember, which we thought was probably good."
   What is "it"? _____

3. "**This place** has an energy that I don't want to lose; it's full of young people who want to change the world as much as I do. That's what I love."
   What is "this place"? _____

4. "We've been through some tough times, but we've never had rough times together. There was hardly ever any tension between **him** and me. It's just a fantastic relationship, and I hope it's a lifelong one."
   Who is "him"? _____

◆ RESPONDING TO THE READING

Answer the questions by putting a check (✓) under *Yes* or *No*.

1. When they were only six months from finishing their doctorates in electrical engineering, Jerry and David abandoned their studies to work on "Jerry's Guide to the World Wide Web." If you were only six months from finishing a university degree, would you quit your studies to do something you were more interested in?
Yes ❏   No ❏

2. Jerry and David worked 20 hours a day on Jerry's list. Would you sit at a computer for hours and hours if you were working on something you were really interested in?
Yes ❏   No ❏

3. Jerry and David didn't accept high-paying jobs with large corporations; instead, they started their own company. If you were offered a high-paying job with a large corporation, would you say "No, thank you" and start your own company instead?
Yes ❏   No ❏

4. Even after Jerry and David became millionaires, their lives didn't change much: David still drove his 1981 Datsun, and Jerry wore a green plastic Yahoo! watch. If you suddenly became a millionaire, would you still drive an old car and wear a cheap plastic watch?
Yes ❏   No ❏

Now compare your answers with a partner's. Explain why you checked *Yes* or *No*. Then count how many times you checked *Yes*. Who is more like Jerry and David, you or your partner?

The woman in the photo is JoMei Chang. Like David Filo and Jerry Yang, Ms. Chang works with computers and started her own company. She told the story below to a newspaper reporter, who wrote it down and published it in the *New York Times*.

In the title of the article, Ms. Chang says, "Calm in crisis is in my blood." What does it mean when someone says a quality is "in my blood"?

Calm in Crisis Is in My Blood, by JoMei Chang

In Chinese the word *crisis* is translated as "dangerous opportunity." When things get bad, I become super creative and super determined. The road I have taken is sometimes bumpy, but the worse the situation is, the calmer and cooler I get. I get that from my mother.

I remember a story my mother told me when I was young. During World War II, she and my grandmother lived in China. They escaped from their hometown and were going to a town that was supposed to be safer, away from the fighting. They took a train, and when the train got to a bridge, bombs started to fall on the train. Everyone on the train went under the bridge for cover. My grandmother could not move easily. She was over 80. My mother was not going to leave her alone on the train, so they sat there. There was nothing they could do. They started to chitchat about ordinary, everyday things while bombs were going off. After the bombing stopped, everyone came back onto the train and was amazed to see them sitting there.

When I got out of graduate school and went to work for Bell Labs as a researcher in the early 1980s, I was terrified. During my first month, I went to a lunch for all the new researchers. The lunch was given by the man who was vice president for research. I knew a lot about him. He was a Nobel Prize winner.

I was sitting in the first row. He was looking at me. I remember that he said, "Don't be afraid to break rules. Rules are made to be broken." Ever since that meeting, I have felt completely free to do whatever I wanted. I stand behind what I believe and never give in.

At a banquet last year, I sat next to a famous football player. The whole table was trying to talk to him. Then they all started talking about Silicon Valley and how easy it was to make money there. I jumped in: "I believe the way to make money is not to focus on making money. Stand behind what you believe, and if you're willing to lose money, then you'll be successful."

(continued)

That statement caught the football player's attention. We talked nonstop for 45 minutes. He said the reason he was a good football player was because he always focused on the task at hand rather than winning or losing.

When my husband and I started our software company, Vitria, we were debating about whether to take venture capital financing. The venture capital firm was going to give us a few million dollars for a stake in our company. I didn't have to risk my money, and I'd be paid a big salary. That sounded pretty good. On the other hand, they didn't fundamentally understand what we wanted to do.

We ended up investing our own money. I never regretted that. ◆

◆ SHARING YOUR TRUE STORIES

Discuss the answers to these questions with your classmates.

1. JoMei Chang says that being calm in a crisis is in her blood. Do you have a quality—for example, being a good cook or loving to swim—that is in your blood? What is that quality?

2. JoMei Chang tells the story of her mother and grandmother being calm in a crisis. Do you have a story about people in your family who were calm in a crisis? Tell the story.

3. JoMei Chang says she is "super creative" and "super determined." What other words and phrases does she use to describe herself? With your classmates, make a list on the board. If you had to describe yourself with only one adjective (any adjective, not just those on the board), which word would you choose? Explain why that adjective fits you.

4. The people quoted in the article give the following advice. After you read their advice, explain why you agree or do not agree.

   ▶ "Don't be afraid to break rules. Rules are made to be broken." (the vice president for research at Bell Labs)

   ▶ "The way to make money is not to focus on making money. Stand behind what you believe, and . . . you'll be successful." (JoMei Chang)

   ▶ "Focus on the task at hand rather than winning or losing." (the football player)

NEWS AND VIEWS

You have read about Jerry Yang, David Filo, and JoMei Chang—three people who know a lot about technology and computers. Do you think these three people probably have some personality traits in common? Do computers and technology attract a certain type of person? Are you one of those people?

Is technology your passion? Are you the one friends call when their computer screens freeze up or when they have lost an important computer file? Do you want to be a computer programmer or Web site designer, or are you already one? Do you work, or want to work, in the technical support department of a corporation, hospital, or university? If you answered "yes" to any of these questions, you might be a geek.

In his book *Geeks*, technology writer Jon Katz describes what a geek is.

As you read, think about this: Does Jon Katz's description of a geek fit you or someone you know?

From *Geeks* by Jon Katz

What is a geek?

1   In the early 1900s, geeks were destitute, homeless men who worked at circuses and carnivals. They bit the heads off chickens and rats in exchange for food or a place to sleep. Later the word "geek" was used to describe anyone who was strange or nonconformist. Then, sometime in the 1990s, the meaning of the word changed again: Today, a geek is someone who is passionate about technology and has a talent for working with computers.

2   I have met and corresponded with thousands of geeks, and I still can't answer the question, "What exactly is a geek?" I can only make some general observations on what today's geeks are, and what they are not.

3   For one thing, geeks are not the asocial loners some people think they are. You can hardly be a geek all by yourself. The on-line world is one giant community comprised of hundreds of thousands of smaller ones, all involving connections to other people. The geekiest hangouts on the Internet are hive-like communities of worker geeks patching together cheap and efficient new software that they share freely and generously with one another. That's not something loners could or would do.

4   Geeks are smart. I've met skinny and fat geeks, shy and outgoing ones, cheerful and grumpy ones—but never dumb ones.

5   Geeks are not like other people. They've grown up in the freest media environment ever. They talk openly about politics and criticize revered leaders. They defy government, business, or any other institution to shut down their freewheeling culture.

Are you a geek?

6   People e-mail me all the time asking if they are geeks.

7   I figure people have the right to name themselves; if you feel like a geek, you are one. But here are some clues: You are on-line a good part of the time. You feel a personal connection with technology, not with the machines themselves, but with what the machines can do. You like to watch *The Simpsons* on TV and you like the *Star Wars* movies. You are obsessive about pop culture, which is what you talk about with your friends or coworkers every Monday.

8   You don't like being told what to do because you believe that people in authority are generally not on your side. Life began for you when you got out of high school, which, more likely than not, was a painful experience. You didn't go to dances, or if you did, you certainly didn't feel comfortable there. Maybe your parents helped you get through, maybe a teacher or a soul mate.

9   Now, you zone out on your work. You solve problems and puzzles. You love to create things just for the kick of it. Even though you're indispensable to the company that's hired you, it's

(continued)

almost impossible to imagine yourself running it. You may have power of your own now—a family, money—yet you see yourself as an outsider, one who never quite fits in. In many ways, geekdom is a state of mind—a sense of yourself in relation to the world.

What does the future hold for geeks?

10   More and more, the world depends on computers and the people who run them. As a result, geeks have almost limitless job prospects. The U.S. Department of Labor predicts that over the next several years the fastest-growing occupations will be in the computer field.

11   Geeks are literally building the new global economy, constructing and expanding the Internet and the World Wide Web as well as maintaining it. They're paid well for their skills: Starting salaries for college grads with computer degrees are high, and the demand is so great that many geeks forgo or abandon college. Elite universities like Caltech, Stanford, and MIT complain that some of their best students abandon graduate school for high-paying positions in technology industries.

12   Until now, geeks were thought to be unglamorous and have never had great status or influence. But the Internet is the hottest and hippest place in American culture, and the people who were formerly outsiders are now insiders. Geeks are often the only ones able to operate our most complex and vital computer systems, and their work will be in demand for years to come.

13   For the first time ever, it's a great time to be a geek. ◆

BUILDING VOCABULARY

◆ UNDERSTANDING ACADEMIC VOCABULARY

The words below are on the Academic Word List.* Find the words in "Geeks."
(The number in parentheses is the number of the paragraph.) If you are not sure
what a word means, look it up in your dictionary. Then use the words in the
sentences that follow.

comprises (3)	**predict** (10)	**expanded** (11)	**abandon** (11)
environment (5)	**global** (11)	**maintain** (11)	**status** (12)
authority (8)	**construct** (11)		

1. When his car broke down, he had to _____ it at the side of the road and walk all the way home.

2. Temperatures are rising all over the world, and many scientists are concerned about _____ warming.

*For an explanation and the complete Academic Word List, see page 157.

3. The city's school system, which _____ two high schools, three middle schools, and four elementary schools, is considered one of the best in the state.

4. She has a lot of power in her position in the company, but she cannot fire workers who are not doing their jobs well; only the president of the company has the _____ to do that.

5. The company has redecorated its offices and installed brighter lighting so that its employees will have a more pleasant _____ in which to work.

6. The highway goes right though the center of the town, but there are plans to _____ a new highway that will go around the town.

7. Some people drive a luxury car so that others know how rich or how important they are. The car is a _____ symbol.

8. The old engine had a lot of moving parts, so it was not easy to take care of. The new engine has fewer moving parts and should be easier to _____.

9. The company used to sell its chocolate only in Switzerland. But over the years, the business _____, and now the chocolate is sold all over Europe.

10. Before a storm, animals often become restless and will not lie down. Some farmers say they can _____ the weather by watching their animals.

◆ **UNDERSTANDING SLANG EXPRESSIONS**

Find the slang expressions in the article. (The number in parentheses is the number of the paragraph.) Then read the expressions in the new contexts below. Finally, complete the definition of each slang expression. The first one is done for you.

a loner (3)   zone out (9)

hangout (3)   just for the kick of it (9)

1. He's a loner. We've invited him to parties, but he never comes. He seems happiest when he's by himself, watching a movie or working at his computer. A "loner" is a person who *prefers to be alone* _____.

2. The swimming pool is a popular hangout. In the summer, a lot of teenagers spend their afternoons there, swimming, talking, and eating snacks. A "hangout" is a place where people _____
_____.

3. I completely zoned out on my work. I forgot to eat lunch and didn't even notice that it had gotten late and the room was getting dark.

If you "zone out" on your work, you _____

_____.

4. Just for the kick of it, we decided to run to the bus stop, even though we had plenty of time to walk.

If you do something "just for the kick of it," you do it _____

_____.

DEVELOPING READING SKILLS

◆ UNDERSTANDING THE MAIN IDEAS

There are three correct ways to complete each sentence. Draw a line through the one incorrect answer.

1. Jon Katz
   a. writes about technology and is the author of a book titled *Geeks*.
   b. ~~knows exactly what a geek is because he is one.~~
   c. has met and corresponded with thousands of geeks.
   d. says he can't answer the question, "What exactly is a geek?"

2. Some definitions of the word *geek* are
   a. poor, homeless men who worked at circuses and carnivals in exchange for food or a place to sleep.
   b. anyone who is strange or nonconformist.
   c. anyone who has extreme political opinions.
   d. someone who is passionate about technology and has a talent for working with computers.

3. When people ask Jon Katz if they are geeks, he
   a. tells them, "You are a geek if you feel like one."
   b. gives them clues that tell them if they are geeks.
   c. tells them what geeks typically do.
   d. tells them that the word *geek* is impossible to define.

4. Today is a great time to be a geek because they
   a. easily get into top universities, like Caltech and MIT.
   b. have almost limitless job prospects.
   c. are paid well for their skills.
   d. are constructing and expanding the Internet, the hottest place in American culture.

◆ UNDERSTANDING DETAILS

The men in the photo above say they are geeks. According to the author of *Geeks,* what are they like, and what do they typically do? On a separate piece of paper, write at least eight sentences that describe these men. For example:

▸ *They talk openly about politics.*

▸ *They are online a lot.*

READING A BAR GRAPH

Slashdot is a Web site for people who are interested in technology. Often there is a question at the Slashdot Web site. Visitors to the site answer the question, and the next day Slashdot reports their answers. (Usually about 50,000 people answer the question.)

On pages 52–54, there are some questions Slashdot asked on its Web site. Read the questions and graphs. Then write a sentence about each graph that tells something about the people who come to the Slashdot Web site. The first one is done for you.

Geeks   **51**

1. What is your gender?

Male	94%
Female	6%

Most of the people who come to Slashdot are male.

2. How old are you?

Under 10	3%
11–17	8%
18–23	40%
24–30	33%
31–40	12%
41–50	3%
51+	1%

3. What is an appliance you can't do without?

Computer	58%
Microwave	4%
Vacuum cleaner	3%
Refrigerator	21%
Television	5%
Home stereo	9%

4. How many computers are in your home?

None	1%
1	12%
2	24%
3	24%
4–5	23%
6+	16%

5. How soon after you wake up do you check your e-mail?

Under 10 minutes	38%
11–30 minutes	21%
31–60 minutes	14%
1–2 hours	18%
2–4 hours	5%
5–8 hours	2%
Longer than 8 hours	2%

6. How many music CDs do you own?

0–10	3%
11–30	6%
31–70	12%
71–100	9%
101–250	23%
251–750	17%
751+	30%

(continued)

7. What is your usual workday?

Less than 8 hours	18%
8 hours	25%
9–10 hours	36%
11–12 hours	12%
13–14 hours	5%
15+ hours	4%

8. What do you wear to work?

Bathrobe	3%
Shorts and a T-shirt	28%
Jeans	43%
Slacks	20%
Suit	6%

DISCUSSION

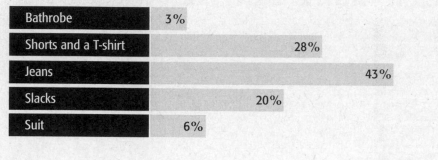 **A** **Below are six statements about geeks. Five of the statements are true, and one is not true. In a small group, read the statements and try to guess which statement is not true. When your group has made its decision, tell the class your guess. Then look on page 155 to find out if your group was right.**

1. The number of women studying computer science is rising dramatically in the United States.

2. Many geeks are making a lot of money but don't have time to spend it.

3. Geeks watch TV less often than most people.

4. Geeks in Silicon Valley are attending etiquette school to learn table manners.

5. Some cruise ship lines are offering special "Geek Cruises" so that geeks can take classes in computer programming while on vacation.

6. Volunteer geeks from many countries are traveling around the world, helping people gain access to information technology.

B 1. **According to Jon Katz, the statements below describe geeks. Read each statement. Check the *Yes* box if the statement describes you and the *No* box if it doesn't.**

	Yes	No
1. You are online a good part of the time.	☐	☐
2. You feel a personal connection with technology.	☐	☐
3. You like popular culture (popular movies, music, TV programs).	☐	☐
4. You don't like being told what to do.	☐	☐
5. You believe that people in authority are not on your side.	☐	☐
6. You like to solve problems and puzzles.	☐	☐
7. You love to create things.	☐	☐
8. You see yourself as an outsider—someone who never quite fits in.	☐	☐

2. **Now discuss the answers to these questions:**

▸ Who in the the class fits Jon Katz's description of a geek?

▸ Who in the class definitely does not fit his description of a geek?

▸ Do you think the statements describe only geeks in the United States, or is there an "international geek"? (To find out, you could give the test to people from three different countries. Did some people answer *Yes* often?)

C **Here are some new words that people who work in technology fields use. (These expressions, called *geek–speak,* are probably not in your dictionary.) In a small group, try to guess the meaning of the expressions. When you are finished guessing, turn to page 155 and read the meaning of each expression.**

1. Ohnosecond   (Hint: Say the word slowly. Say, "Oh . . . no . . . second.")

2. Facemail   (Hint: How is facemail different from e-mail?)

3. Eye candy   (Hint: Candy is something good to eat, so eye candy must be something good to _____.)

4. Treeware   (Hint: What is made from trees?)

5. Virus   (Hint: A cold is an example of a virus that spreads quickly from person to person.)

6. 24/7   (Hint: People in technology fields often work more than 40 hours a week.)

WRITING

Choose one of the following topics to write about.

1. Jerry Yang is athletic (not a typical geek characteristic) and was popular in high school (not a typical geek characteristic). So, he is described as "not a typical geek." Can anyone really be described as a typical anything? Can you say, for example, that someone is a typical athlete, a typical artist, or a typical American? Explain your answer.

2. Jerry Yang and David Filo's story is called a "rags-to-riches" story. Because of Yahoo!'s success, they went from having no money to having a lot of money. Do you know a rags-to-riches story? Tell the story in writing.

3. Jon Katz writes that geeks feel a personal connection with technology. What are your feelings about machines and services that are the result of new technology, such as computers, e-mail, answering machines, and cell phones? Choose one machine or service and explain what you like or don't like about it.

4. Jon Katz believes that it's a great time to be a geek. Is it a great time to be a geek in your country? Explain why it is or isn't.

5. Are you a geek? Explain why you are or aren't.

Finding The Right Person To Marry

Have you already found the person you want to marry? Or are you still looking for the right person?

Read the following statements about love and marriage. Write *Yes* on the line if you agree with the statement. Write *No* on the line if you disagree.

_____ 1. "True love" comes to you only once in your lifetime.

_____ 2. "Love at first sight" can happen.

_____ 3. It is possible for old people (older than 75) to fall in love.

_____ 4. It is very important that your husband or wife is your "soul mate"—your best friend and partner, someone who understands you.

_____ 5. The most important reason to get married is to have children.

_____ 6. It is important for a woman to marry a man who can make enough money to support a family.

_____ 7. It is important to marry someone who shares your religion.

_____ 8. Choosing the person you marry is the most important decision of your life.

Share your answers with the class. Did the people in your class respond to the statements in the same way?

In this unit, you will first read a true story about two couples who unexpectedly found love on a cruise ship. Next, you will read the responses of four international students who were asked, "What are you looking for in a husband or wife?" Finally, you will find out what young adults in the United States are looking for in a spouse.

PRE-READING

Look at the photo and read the title of the story on the next page. With your classmates, make a list of questions you think the story will answer.

Example:

▸ *How did the people in the picture meet?*

▸ *Are the older people the parents of the younger people?*

When you have finished reading the story, look back at the questions you and your classmates wrote. Which questions did the story answer?

Shipmates and Soul Mates
by Elizabeth Leland

1   Unable to sleep, Mary Aaronson got out of bed in the middle of the night and walked out of her lonely house. She lived on the coast of England, and from the garden of her house she could see the Atlantic Ocean. She gazed out over the ocean and then looked up to find the brightest star in the sky. Night after night, she talked to the star as if she were talking to her husband. "Edward! I don't like being on my own!"

2   Edward, Mary's husband, had died of lung cancer, and Mary couldn't remember how to live without him. She missed dancing in his arms on Saturday nights. She missed walking hand in hand with him through the English countryside. She missed picnicking by his side on the cliffs overlooking the sea.

3   She was 63 years old and living alone for the first time in her life. She confided in her daughter, Moya, that she was terribly lonely. "Let's take a holiday," her daughter suggested.

4   Half a world away, in Charlotte, North Carolina, Merritt Burns also found it impossible to sleep. He knelt by his bed and prayed. He took sleeping pills. When the pills didn't work, he'd walk the streets of Charlotte for hours.

5   During the day, he tried to shut the world out. He closed the curtains in his house, stopped the newspaper, cut off the cable TV. Often his son would visit and find him sitting in the dark. "How did your day go?" his son would ask. "I've been just sitting here," he would answer, "hoping that nobody would call or come by."

6   Merritt had lost his wife, Lydia, to cancer after 54 years of marriage. He was 76 years old and he wanted to die.

7   "Let's take a vacation together," his son, David, pleaded.

8   And so, Merritt Burns and his son, David, flew to the western coast of Canada and boarded a cruise ship bound for Alaska. Mary Aaronson and her daughter, Moya, flew from England and boarded the same ship.

9   On the first night of the cruise, the four were seated together at the dinner table. Mary and Merritt hit it off immediately. They talked about North Carolina and England, about their families, about the seven-day cruise. They laughed a lot—something they both needed desperately to do. When Mary invited Merritt to go sightseeing with her when the ship docked in Alaska, Merritt immediately said yes.

10   As Mary and Merritt walked through the streets of Juneau, Alaska, Mary took Merritt's hand. They walked hand in hand the rest of the day.

11   That night, Merritt confided in his son. "Oh, I could have a lot of fun with her. She's brilliant." But Merritt had known Mary such a short time. Was he getting carried away? "Maybe this is just a silly infatuation—at my age!" Merritt said.

12   "Enjoy it, Dad," David told him.

13   Meanwhile, Mary was confiding in her daughter. "He makes my heart go flutter!" To her daughter, Mary seemed like altogether a different person, no longer a lonely widow. She looked radiant, cheeks flushed, hazel eyes sparkling. "Do you think I'm making a fool of myself at my time of life?" Mary asked.

14   "No, Mum. Go for it," Moya told her.

15   Mary and Moya talked mostly about Merritt. But they also talked about Merritt's son David. David and Moya were both single—David was divorced, and Moya had never married—and Mary had noticed that David seemed to be flirting with Moya.

16   "David's so nice," Mary said.

17   "He's not the one for me," Moya answered.

(continued)

18   David was worrying so much about his father and still grieving for his mother that he kept his personality hidden. He was quiet and subdued. Whenever Merritt wasn't with Mary, David was by his side, a 48-year-old man following his father everywhere.

19   Once David and Moya were together on the deck of the cruise ship. A little girl walked up to them and asked, "Are you married?"

20   "Married?" Moya said, and laughed. "We're practically brother and sister!"

21   When the cruise ended, Mary and Moya flew back to England, and Merritt and David flew back to North Carolina. Every day Merritt called Mary from North Carolina, where it was 5 P.M., to wish her good night. Three months later, he flew to England to visit her. Walking hand in hand with Mary through the English countryside, Merritt knew he'd met his soul mate. Without warning, Merritt lifted Mary off her feet and sat her down on a rock. At 5 feet 11 inches, 180 pounds, he was still strong at 76. "You sit here," he said. "I'm going to sing you a love song."

22   "Be my love, for no one else can end this yearning," Merritt sang.

23   Mary looked around her. She could see people walking their way. "What will people think of me sitting up here on this rock with Merritt below, belting out a love song?" she wondered.

24   That night over dinner at a pub,[1] Merritt and Mary talked of marriage. "Look," he told her. "I'm old. I've got one foot in the grave. I can just see us getting married and my breaking down and you having to take care of me."

25   "Well, if you'll take me just as I am," Mary said, "I'll take you just as you are. We'll grow old together."

26   Mary and Merritt decided to get married in North Carolina. After Mary left England to prepare for the wedding, it was Moya's turn to feel lonely. Her father had died and her mother was 4,000 miles away across an ocean. Alone in the dark, she sat on the floor of her house and sobbed.

27   Moya flew to the United States for her mother's wedding in the company of two of her aunts. There to meet them at the airport were David and Merritt. It felt good to Moya to have so much family around, to be held close by people who cared. As they walked to the car, Moya took David's hand. That simple gesture, which came so naturally to Moya that day, surprised David. Yet he was excited about what it might mean.

28   David seemed like a different person to Moya. No longer worried about his father, he was light-hearted and funny. He made her laugh so much, tears rolled down her cheeks. The week she stayed in North Carolina for her mother's wedding, Moya spent by David's side.

29   Now it was David and Moya who acted like teenagers falling in love. As Moya's mother walked down the church aisle to marry David's father, Moya nudged David and said, "Maybe we should knock them out of the way and say, 'Wait! It's our turn!'" David grinned.

30   After her mother's wedding, Moya went back to England, but three months later she returned to the United States to spend more time with David. She realized that he was the one for her after all. When David asked Moya to marry him, she said yes.

31   David and Moya, like their parents, married in North Carolina. After their wedding, they drove to the cemetery where David's mother was buried. David placed Moya's wedding bouquet on his mother's grave. "Mom, this is Moya," David said quietly.

32   David and Merritt have not forgotten Lydia Burns, wife and mother, who died in 1996. Nor have Moya and Mary forgotten Edward Aaronson, husband and father, who died in 1995. Lydia and Edward are still thought about, still missed, still loved. The legacy of their lives is the love that bloomed between Merritt and Mary, David and Moya.

33   It was almost as if, from wherever they were, they had planned it all. ◆

---

[1] **pub** = a comfortable bar that often serves food

GETTING THE BIG PICTURE

Circle the letter of your answer.

The people in the photo on page 58 are happy because they

a. are enjoying a beautiful cruise.

b. were all alone but now have love in their lives.

c. were separated but are now together.

BUILDING VOCABULARY

◆ **RECALLING NEW WORDS**

Which words have the same meaning as the underlined words from the story? Circle the letter of the correct answer.

1. Mary's husband had died, and she was living alone for the first time in her life. She was <u>terribly</u> lonely.
   a. very
   b. a little

2. David knew that his father wanted to die. <u>He pleaded with him to take a vacation.</u>
   a. "Please, *please* take a vacation," he said with emotion.
   b. "I think it would be a good idea to take a vacation," he said casually.

3. During their first dinner together, Merritt and Mary talked and laughed. They <u>hit it off</u> immediately.
   a. asked each other questions
   b. became friends

4. Merritt and Mary had both been very sad, but now they were laughing—something they both needed <u>desperately</u> to do.
   a. very much
   b. sometimes

5. Merritt thought that his conversations with Mary were interesting. "She's <u>brilliant</u>," he said.
   a. very intelligent
   b. very funny

6. After a day of sightseeing with Mary, Merritt began thinking about a future with her. He wondered if he <u>was getting carried away</u>.
   a. was losing control of himself because he was excited
   b. should take another cruise because he was enjoying this one very much

7. Merritt had known Mary only a short time. He was afraid his feelings for her were just <u>a silly infatuation</u>.
   a. a deep sympathy he felt for Mary because she had lost her husband
   b. a foolish love that would not last long

8. <u>Mary confided in her daughter</u>. She told her, "Merritt makes my heart go flutter!"
   a. Mary told her daughter some personal things she did not want other people to know.
   b. Mary told her daughter some news she wanted all her friends and relatives to know.

9. David's mother had died, and he was still <u>grieving</u>.
   a. feeling very sad and upset
   b. feeling a little sad

10. After Mary left for North Carolina, it was Moya's turn to feel sad and lonely. She sat on the floor of her house and <u>sobbed</u>.
    a. planned her future
    b. cried loudly

11. After their wedding, David placed Moya's <u>bouquet</u> on his mother's grave.
    a. ring
    b. bunch of flowers

◆ **USING NEW WORDS**

Complete the sentences with examples from your own life. In small groups, take turns reading your sentences aloud. Ask your classmates questions about their sentences.

1. Children plead with their parents when _____.

2. A person many people in my native country believe is (or was) brilliant is

   _____.

3. I desperately need to _____.

4. The person I confide in most is _____.

5. In my country, people often give a bouquet to someone who _____

   _____.

DEVELOPING READING SKILLS

◆ **UNDERSTANDING THE MAIN IDEAS**

Imagine that a friend points to the photo on page 63 and asks you, "Who are these people?" What would you say about each person? Write your answer on the line. The first one is done for you.

1. _His name is Merritt Burns. He's 76 years old, and he's from North Carolina._
   His wife died of cancer, and he was very lonely—so lonely he wanted to die.
   His son invited him to go on a cruise to Alaska. On the cruise he met Mary,
   the woman next to him in the photo. They fell in love and got married.

2. _____
   _____
   _____
   _____

3. _____
   _____
   _____
   _____

4. _____
   _____
   _____
   _____

◆ **UNDERSTANDING WHERE A STORY TAKES PLACE**

Write the name of the place on the line. The first one is done for you.

1. Mary's house is on the coast of this country. _____England_____

2. Merritt lives in this city. _____

3. The cruise ship departed from this country. _____

4. Merritt and Mary walked hand in hand through the streets of this city in
   Alaska. _____

5. Merritt sang a love song to Mary in the countryside of this country.
   _____

6. At a pub in this country, Merritt and Mary talked about getting married.
   _____

7. Both couples got married in this U.S. state. _____

◆ MAKING INFERENCES ABOUT CULTURE

To *infer* is to use information you have to make a logical guess. When we read about people from other countries, we can make inferences about their cultures by noticing what they say and do. For example, in the story Mary takes Merritt's hand to show him she likes him, and later Moya takes David's hand to show him she likes him. Both Mary and Moya are from England, so we can infer that taking someone's hand is a sign of affection in England. We cannot be sure that is true, but it is a logical guess.

Use information from the story to guess the answers to the questions below. Write your answer on the line.

1. What do some older married couples do in their free time in England?
   They go dancing, walking, and picnicking.

2. What do some people in the United States do when they can't sleep?

   _____

3. What might a person in the United States do if he or she didn't want any contact with the outside world?

   _____

4. In England and the United States, what might adult children do with a grieving parent to help the parent feel better?

   _____

5. Where do people in England sometimes go for a meal or a drink?

   _____

6. In what building do people in the United States sometimes get married?

   _____

Merritt Burns and Mary Aaronson fell in love on a cruise ship. Merritt thought Mary was "brilliant," and Mary said Merritt made her heart beat fast. What are you looking for in a spouse? Are you looking for someone who is brilliant? Are you looking for someone who makes your heart beat fast?

The people below, all students at a university in the United States, were asked what they are looking for in a husband or wife. Read what they said.

What Are You Looking for in a Spouse?

Name: Burim
Country: Kosovo
Age: 27

Name: Zsofi
Country: Hungary
Age: 25

I think it will be better to find someone from my country, who is from the same culture and has the same traditions, the same religion . . . someone who will respect me, my family, and my friends. She will be from the same place, and she will understand me more.

I don't plan to find a girl, get married, see if it works, and then if it doesn't, get divorced, which I see many people here in the United States do. That's why I would like to find a religious girl, exactly the girl I am looking for, and then live my whole life with her.

I know for certain that I would only marry someone I had known for a few years. You can come across some surprises if you trust yourself too much and make judgments too quickly.

If I ever get married, I definitely will marry somebody whom I can look up to and who will never let me be too wishy-washy. I love the differences between the two genders, but as time passes men are becoming very woman-like. My husband has to be a man who can stand on his own two feet.

(continued)

Name: Aldo
Country: Brazil
Age: 22

Name: Kanjana
Country: Thailand
Age: 24

I don't want my wife and me to be too independent. Couples in the United States are so independent, they can get everything by themselves. But then after they have a fight, they can just say, "Why should we stay together? One of us can move." In my culture, people struggle and have to depend on one other. When couples have a fight, they have to put up with each other. That's why marriages in Brazil last longer.

I'm looking for someone who can complete me. I don't want someone who can do pretty much the same things I can. I'm not saying that she has to cook and I have to cut the grass. If I like to cook and she likes to fix computers, that's OK. Some things my wife should know how to do better than me, and some things I should know how to do better than her.

I think it's important to find someone who wants to have children. When people get married, they should have children because children can take care of us when we're older. It's hard to find someone who loves us as much as our children do.

I also think it's important for the man to have enough money. If the woman can earn money, that's good, too, but it's more important that the man earns enough because he is the leader of the family. But if I had to choose between a man who has a lot of money and a man who understands me and loves me, I would choose the one who loves me. ◆

◆ **SHARING YOUR TRUE STORIES**

Discuss the answers to these questions with your classmates.

1. Are any of the opinions expressed above similar to your own? Give reasons for your opinions. If you have a story to support an opinion, tell it to your classmates. (For example, do you, like Burim, want to marry someone from your country? Why? Do you know two people from different countries who got married and had problems? Tell the class the story.)

2. What would you answer if someone asked you, "What are you looking for in a spouse?" (If you are already married, what would you answer if someone asked you, "What were you looking for in a spouse?") Explain your answer.

NEWS AND VIEWS

You have read the responses of four international students to the question, "What are you looking for in a spouse?" Then you thought about how you would answer that question. Now you will learn what most young adults in the United States are looking for in a husband or wife. The information comes from a survey done at Rutgers University in New Jersey.

Before you read the article, try to predict what the survey showed. Read each statement below. Write *Yes* if you agree with the statement and *No* if you disagree.

_____ 1. Young adults in the United States are probably looking for the same qualities the four international students are looking for.

_____ 2. They are probably looking for the same qualities their parents and grandparents were looking for.

_____ 3. They are probably looking for the same qualities I am (or was) looking for.

Now read the article to find out what the survey actually showed.

Who Wants to Marry a Soul Mate?

1   What are young adults in the United States looking for in a spouse? Are they looking for a person who will be a great father or mother someday? No. Are they looking for someone who will help them financially? No. Are they looking for someone who shares their religion? Most say no. What, then, are they looking for in a husband or wife? They are looking for someone who is, above all, their "soul mate"—someone who is their best friend and partner, someone who understands them, someone with whom they have a deep emotional connection.

2   That information comes from a recent telephone survey of 1,000 Americans ages 20 to 29. Researchers at Rutgers University called young men and women living in the eastern United States and read statements about marriage. The young adults were asked to reply "yes" if they agreed with the

statement and "no" if they disagreed. Here, for example, are a few of the statements:

- The main purpose of marriage is to have children.
- A woman should not rely on marriage for financial security.
- It is important to find a spouse who shares your religion.

To the surprise of the researchers, the statement receiving the largest percentage of "yes" responses, with 94 percent agreeing, was: "When you marry, you want your spouse to be your soul mate, first and foremost."

3   Sociologists say these results indicate that in the United States young adults' attitudes toward marriage are different from those of their grandparents and great-grandparents. Many of the social, economic, and religious reasons for marrying and choosing a spouse that were important to previous generations

(continued)

are no longer important. In the past, for example, many people believed the purpose of marriage was to have children—to create a family. Only 16 percent of young adults questioned in the survey believe that "the main purpose of marriage is to have children." In earlier generations, most women saw marriage as a way to become economically independent from their parents and financially secure. Today, a young woman is more likely to rely on herself financially, believing that her own education and career—not her husband's—will give her economic independence and security. Not long ago, most people in the United States thought it was very important to marry someone of the same religion. Today, only 42 percent of young adults believe this.

4   Replacing yesterday's social, economic, and religious reasons for marrying are reasons that are romantic, perhaps even naive or unrealistic. Today's young adults want, more than anything else, to have togetherness, support, and closeness in their marriages; they want a "super-relationship" between two people, rather than a relationship that is just one of many close relationships they have.

5   Some sociologists believe that young people in the U.S. may be looking for this "super-relationship" because they do not have many other relationships that are strong and lasting. Contemporary U.S. society is mobile—many people move as often as every seven years—and the pace of life is frantic. Those two factors make it difficult to have deep and lasting relationships. In addition, the divorce rate is high in the United States; 43 percent of all marriages end. So, young adults may be looking for the emotional support and comfort that is missing from other parts of their lives.

6   Hayley Kaufman, a reporter at the *Boston Globe* who is in her late 20s, agrees that the high divorce rate may explain her generation's search for a soul mate. In a *Boston Globe* article, she writes:

7   While the soul-mate idea may have older Americans shaking their heads and laughing, it makes perfect sense to those of us who are in our twenties and thirties. We're the ones, after all, who watched our parents split up and our friends' parents split up.

8   By the mid-1980s, as the American divorce rate was peaking at 50 percent, our lives had been marked by events our parents never could have dreamed of when they were kids. We sat through family-therapy sessions before getting dropped off at school puffy-eyed and sniffling. We woke up one morning to discover that Dad had packed a suitcase and moved into an apartment. At the tender age of 10, we carried around two different sets of house keys—one set for Mom's house, another set for Dad's.

9   Even if our parents decided to stick it out, many of our friends' parents didn't. We watched as parent after parent moved out and, frequently, remarried. We were the ones who got the phone calls after our depressed, angry, and just plain sad adolescent friends had just eaten a holiday dinner with a bunch of steprelatives they barely knew.

10   The people we saw split up weren't soul mates—not by a long shot. Surely they'd been in love at some point. But they got married for a lot of other reasons. They wanted a provider. Or someone who shared the same religion. Or a good mother for their kids. Or they thought it was just time.

11   It's no wonder young Americans want a soul mate. After a lifetime of broken bonds, we're all hoping for one relationship that will last.

12   The survey seems to support Ms. Kaufman's belief that her generation is looking for "one relationship that will last." When researchers read this statement: "It is unlikely that I will stay married to the same person for life," only 6 percent of young adults agreed. In other words, 94 percent of the people who participated in the survey intend to stay married to their "soul mates" for their entire lives.

13   Older adults—even the ones shaking their heads and laughing at the "soul mate" idea—wish them well and hope they do. ◆

BUILDING ACADEMIC VOCABULARY

The words below are on the Academic Word List.* Find the words in "Who Wants to Marry a Soul Mate?" (The number in parentheses is the number of the paragraph.) If you are not sure what a word means, look it up in your dictionary. Then use the words in the sentences that follow.

financially (1)	**previous** (3)	**created** (3)	**bond** (11)
attitude (3)	**generations** (3)	**secure** (3)	**participated** (12)
economic (3)		**rely on** (3)	

1. Some people believe that the universe began with a big explosion, but others do not believe it was _____ in that way.

2. If your car always starts and never breaks down, you have a car you can _____.

3. A photo of a woman with her daughter, granddaughter, and great-granddaughter shows four _____ in a family.

4. Most job applications ask for information about work experience you've had. You usually have to list all your _____ employers.

5. He has a close relationship with his cousin, but the _____ with his brother is even stronger.

6. When she was in high school, she played soccer and belonged to several clubs; all together, she _____ in four after-school activities.

7. Small children stay close to their mothers, where they feel safe and _____.

8. Students who hated school but like it now had a change in _____.

9. Someone who loans you money helps you out _____.

10. If a country's unemployment rate is high—that is, if a lot of people can't find work—the country's _____ situation is not good.

DEVELOPING READING SKILLS

◆ UNDERSTANDING THE MAIN IDEAS

There are three correct ways to complete each sentence. Draw a line through the one incorrect answer.

1. A recent survey indicates that young adults in the United States want to marry a "soul mate." A soul mate is someone
   a. with whom you have a deep emotional connection.
   b. who understands you.
   c. ~~who will help you financially.~~
   d. who is your best friend and partner.

*For an explanation and the complete Academic Word List, see page 157.

2. The survey was conducted in this way:

   a. Researchers at Rutgers University in the United States telephoned 1,000 Americans ages 20 to 29.
   b. The researchers read statements about marriage.
   c. The young adults responded "yes" if they agreed with the statement and "no" if they disagreed.
   d. The researchers asked the young adults to describe what they were looking for in a spouse.

3. In the past, many people believed that

   a. the purpose of marriage was to have children.
   b. marriage was a way for a woman to become financially secure.
   c. it was very important to marry someone of the same religion.
   d. marriage was hard work and a full-time job.

4. Some young adults in the United States do not have many deep and lasting relationships because

   a. in the United States, work is more important than friends and family.
   b. people move often, making it difficult to make friends.
   c. the frantic pace of life leaves no time for friends.
   d. family members become separated when parents divorce.

5. Hayley Kaufman, a reporter at the *Boston Globe*, writes that

   a. the divorce rate was at 50 percent when she was growing up.
   b. many couples in her parents' generation married not for love but for other reasons.
   c. the "soul mate" idea makes perfect sense to her generation.
   d. she has already found her soul mate.

◆ SEPARATING FACT FROM OPINION

The ability to separate a fact from an opinion is an important reading skill. A *fact* is information that is known to be true or can be proven. For example, this statement is a fact: "In the United States, the average age for men to marry is 27, and for women it is 25." Opinions are people's ideas and beliefs and cannot be proven. This statement is an opinion: "Men should not get married until they are at least 25 years old."

Read the following sentences from the article. If you think the sentence gives you a fact, write *F* on the line. If you think the sentence gives you an opinion, write *O* on the line.

___F___ 1. Researchers at Rutgers University in the United States conducted a telephone survey of 1,000 Americans ages 20 to 29.

_____ 2. It is important to find a spouse who shares your religion.

_____ 3. The main purpose of marriage is to have children—to create a family.

_____ 4. Ninety-four percent of the people who participated in the survey say they want their spouse to be their soul mate.

_____ 5. A woman should not rely on marriage for financial security.

_____ 6. Young adults in the United States want to marry for reasons that are romantic—perhaps even naive or unrealistic.

_____ 7. Contemporary U.S. society is mobile: Many people move as often as every seven years.

_____ 8. In the mid-1980s, the American divorce rate was peaking at 50 percent.

READING A BAR GRAPH

You learned in the article "Who Wants to Marry a Soul Mate?" that researchers telephoned people in the United States ages 20 to 29 to find out what they thought about marriage. Below are some statements from the survey and the percentages of people agreeing with them. The percentages are presented in a bar graph.

A Respond to the survey. Read each statement. Write *Yes* on the line if you agree and *No* if you disagree. (If you are already married, answer the questions as you would have answered them before you were married.) Then look at the bar graph to see how your opinions compare with the opinions of the people who participated in the survey.

SURVEY OF BELIEFS ABOUT MARRIAGE

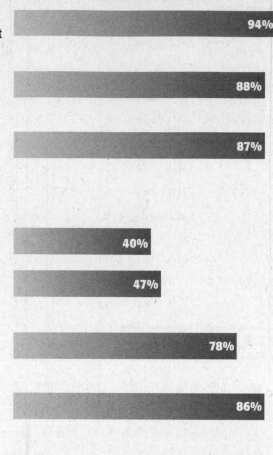

Percent of all men and women
ages 20–29 agreeing

Soul Mates

_____ 1. When you marry, you want your spouse to be your soul mate, first and foremost.

94%

_____ 2. You think that there is a special person, a soul mate, waiting for you somewhere out there.

88%

_____ 3. You think that you will find that special someone when you are ready to get married.

87%

Divorce

_____ 4. Parents should stay together for the sake of their children.

40%

_____ 5. Divorce laws in the U.S. should be changed so that divorces are much more difficult to get.

47%

_____ 6. A couple should not get married unless they are prepared to stay together for life.

78%

_____ 7. Marriage is hard work and a full-time job.

86%

Economic Independence

_____ 8. It is extremely important to you to have enough money before you get married.

86%

_____ 9. Your education or career is more important than marriage at this time in your life.

80%

_____ 10. A woman should not rely on marriage for financial security.

82%

(The next statement is for women only.)

_____ 11. It is more important to have a husband who can communicate about his deepest feelings than to have a husband who makes a good living.

80%

B ▸ **Discuss the answers to these questions with your classmates.**

1. Compare your answers to the survey with those of a classmate. Which of your answers are the same? Which are different? Explain why you answered the way you did.

2. Do you think young adults in your native country would give the same answers that young adults in the United States did? Circle the statements you think young people in your native country would answer very differently. Show the statements you circled to a classmate from a different country. Did you circle the same statements?

C ▸ **Use the statements from the survey on page 72 to conduct your own survey. Follow the steps below.**

1. First, decide who will participate in your survey. For example, you could survey a group of other students from your country. If you decide to survey people who are already married, you will need to change or omit some of the statements.

2. Conduct the survey as the researchers did, asking people to respond "yes" if they agree with the statements and "no" if they disagree.

3. Record the results of your survey as percentages. Compare the results of your survey with the results of the survey on page 72. You can summarize your results in an oral report, in a short essay, or in a bar graph.

DISCUSSION

A ▸ **1. Read below about the four ways to find a soul mate and rate them from 1 to 4 (1 = it's a great idea, and 4 = it's a terrible idea).**

_____ 1. An online dating service

There are over 2,500 Web sites that help people find love on the Internet, and two million people are registered at some of the most popular sites. This is how most of the Web sites work: First, you fill out a questionnaire in which you describe yourself. You might also include a photo of yourself or a short audio clip. Then computers search for people who might be a good match for you—someone, for example, who shares your religion, race, values, or interests. The online dating service then sends you a list of possible matches. It is up to you to contact the people on the list. There is a monthly fee for online dating services, although the first week is free at many sites.

_____ 2. The Lovegety

Currently for sale in Japan, the Lovegety is a plastic gadget people wear around their necks. The Lovegety has a small computer in it. Lovegetys ask their owners what they want to do: have fun, dance, fall in love, see a movie, chat, or meet for a drink. The owners press a button to give their answers. When a woman wearing a Lovegety passes a man wearing a Lovegety, the Lovegetys beep if the two people have chosen the same answers. It is up to the people wearing the beeping Lovegetys to introduce themselves and make a date to meet again.

_____ 3. SpeedDating

SpeedDating (also called Nanodating) began in Los Angeles. The idea spread across the United States and then around the world—to Canada, to Britain, to the Ukraine, and to Australia. The evening begins with an equal number of men and women pairing off to chat for exactly eight minutes. When a bell rings, everyone moves to a different chair to talk to another person for exactly eight minutes. At the end of the evening, men and women tell the organizers which people they would like to see again, and, if both sides agree, phone numbers are given out.

_____ 4. Coffee shop dating

At a network of coffee shops in New York City, you can pay $10 to fill out a form that helps you describe yourself. Then you look through binders filled with thousands of forms. You choose possible soul mates from the binder and tell a staff person who your choices are. The staff person will show your form to the people you have chosen. If they are interested in meeting you, a coffee shop staff person schedules a date—at the coffee shop, of course. One matchmaking service/coffee house, Manhattan's Drip Cafe, has arranged 70 marriages so far.

2. Now compare your ratings with those of your classmates. Explain why you gave each idea the rating you did. Would you consider trying any of these ways to find a soul mate? If so, which ones?

B **1. What do you think of this way to find a soul mate? Read this true story about a man named Tom.**

Tom was experimenting with a computer program. The program lets people select facial features—a nose, eyes, a mouth, a chin—and puts them together to create a picture of a person. Just for fun, Tom decided to create the face of his "dream girl." Tom's problem is that he fell in love with the face he created. Using the Internet, he is trying to find a woman who looks like his "dream girl." Look at the picture on page 75 and read the message he posted:

Have you seen this girl?

My name is Tom Kraemer. I created the picture of the girl above on a computer. She does not actually exist. Since creating the picture, I have fallen in love with the girl in the image. Perhaps this doesn't make sense to you, but I believe I have created the image of my soul mate. She is my "dream girl." I know this might sound strange, but I have to find the girl who matches this image. I know my dream girl, my soul mate, is out there somewhere. Have you seen her? Do you know her? PLEASE have her contact me. My happiness depends on it. Thank you.

2. Now discuss the answers to these questions with your classmates.

▶ What do you think are Tom's chances of finding a woman who looks like the one in the picture? (Look on page 155 to read about his progress so far.)

▶ If Tom finds his "dream girl," what do you think their chances are for being happy together?

▶ After Tom created the picture of his "dream girl," he fell in love with her. Do you believe in love at first sight? Has it happened to you or to someone you know? Tell the class the story.

▶ Tom knows exactly what he wants his soul mate to look like. What about you? Are you attracted to a person who looks a certain way—to someone who is tall, for example, or who has a big smile? Look through magazines to find photos of people who are your "dream men" or "dream women." Show the photos to your classmates and explain why you chose the photos you did.

▶ Tom is looking for a soul mate who looks like the picture. Do you think looks are important in finding a soul mate? What other qualities are important? With your classmates, make a list of important qualities. Write your list on the board.

▶ Separate into two groups, men and women. The women will go to one room, and the men will go to another room. From the list of qualities you and your classmates wrote on the board, each group will choose the five qualities they think are most important in choosing a spouse. Then the groups will come back together. Did the men and women choose the same qualities? If not, why do you think they didn't?

WRITING

Choose one of the following topics to write about.

1. Do you want your spouse to be your soul mate, first and foremost? Explain your answer.

2. Re-read the statements in the survey on page 72. Find a statement with which you strongly agree, or find a statement with which you strongly disagree. Explain why you agree or disagree with the statement.

3. At matchmaking Web sites, people try to find love on the Internet. First, they fill out a form that helps them describe themselves. (They give their eye color, height, religion, occupation, etc.) Then they write an essay with a maximum length of 400 words. The instructions for writing the essay are: "Describe yourself and your personality." There is a list of "helpful questions to get you started." Read the following questions found on one matchmaking Web site. Then choose one of the questions and answer it.

   ▶ How would your best friend describe your personality?

   ▶ What do you like to do for fun?

   ▶ What types of music move you?

   ▶ When are you the happiest?

   ▶ When are you most at peace?

   ▶ What have you done that makes you proud?

   ▶ If you could choose a super power, what would it be?

   ▶ If you could invite any five people (living or dead) to dinner, who would they be?

   ▶ What's your idea of a perfect date?

   ▶ Do you believe in love at first sight? Why or why not?

   ▶ What are you looking for in an ideal mate?

Intuition

The theme of this unit is "intuition." Intuition is the ability to know something or understand something by using your feelings instead of carefully considering all the facts. Do you use your intuition often? Take the quiz below to find out.

Answer each question by putting a check (✓) in the box.	Never	Rarely	Sometimes	Frequently
1. When the doorbell or phone rings unexpectedly, do you know who is there?	❑	❑	❑	❑
2. Have you ever thought about someone you haven't thought of for months and then received a letter or phone call from that person?	❑	❑	❑	❑
3. Do you ever dream about unusual events which actually occur later?	❑	❑	❑	❑
4. Have you ever made a mistake and later realized you had sensed at that time it wasn't the right thing to do?	❑	❑	❑	❑
5. Do your first impressions of people turn out to be accurate?	❑	❑	❑	❑

Score your quiz.
Give yourself:
0 points for each time you checked "never"
1 point for each time you checked "rarely"
2 points for each time you checked "sometimes"
3 points for each time you checked "frequently"

Add up your points. **0–4 points** = You rarely use your intuition; **5–9 points** = You sometimes use your intuition; **10–15 points** = You use your intuition often.

In this unit, you will read about a woman whose intuition led her to an important scientific discovery. Next, you will read the true story of a man whose intuition saved his son's life. Finally, you will learn how psychologists define intuition and how you can learn to use your own intuition.

PRE-READING

Look at the photo and think about these questions. Discuss your answers with your classmates.

▶ Do you know anything about the skeleton in the photo?

▶ Who could the woman in the photo be?

▶ The story on the next page is about the discovery of an important skeleton, and the theme of this unit is "intuition." How could the discovery of a skeleton have anything to do with intuition? What is your guess?

A Sixth Sense

1   Because of a flat tire, Sue Hendrickson found the bones that made her famous.

2   Sue Hendrickson was with a small group of fossil hunters in South Dakota. They had been digging for dinosaur bones all summer, and the dig had been productive. But now it was time to pack up camp and head home. Then, two days before they planned on leaving, the team woke up to find one of the tires on their truck flat and the spare tire low on air. Sue's colleagues headed to a repair station in town, and she stayed behind to continue packing. As she worked, she kept thinking about a small cliff she had seen while exploring nearby ranchland earlier that summer. Her intuition had told her to take a closer look at the cliff, but she hadn't found time to do it. This was her last chance.

3   Sue and her dog, a golden retriever named Gypsy, took a seven-mile walk to the cliff. Sue started looking around its base, and within minutes she spotted some pieces of bone. "Because the bone pieces seemed to have fallen from above, I looked up," Sue says. "About seven feet up the cliff face, three vertebrae were sticking out of the dirt. They were huge—each was the size of a dinner plate. By their shape, I knew the bones had come from a meat-eating dinosaur. And by their size, I knew it could only be a Tyrannosaurus rex— the rarest of all dinosaurs. I started to cry—I was very emotional."

4   For the next three weeks, the team worked 14-hour days digging out the dinosaur skeleton, which they named "Sue" in honor of its discoverer. "Sue" turned out to be the most complete Tyrannosaurus skeleton ever found—and the most valuable. After a long court battle, it was ultimately sold at auction for over $8 million.

5   Scientists were not surprised when they learned that Sue Hendrickson had discovered the 67-million-year-old bones. She is famous in the scientific world for having a sixth sense—an almost supernatural ability to find amazing things. She has discovered precious 23-million-year-old butterflies, sunken ships holding Ming Dynasty vases, Napoleon's sunken warships, and Cleopatra's palace, which was submerged in water near Egypt. She has found treasure chests of gold.

6   Even as a child, Sue had a talent for finding things. "I was always walking with my head down," she says. "I'd go up and down the streets near my house, looking for treasure. I even went through garbage cans looking for stuff."

7   Sue was very bright, but she quit high school when she was 17 to see what was beyond the limits of her small hometown. She traveled around the United States for years, supporting herself with whatever work she could find. In Maine, she got a job diving for lobsters, and she discovered she was good at finding them. ("I could think like a lobster," she says.) In Florida, she convinced two men who collected tropical fish professionally to let her dive with them, and she found out she was good at that, too. From diving for fish she went to diving for sunken boats and then to diving for historical shipwrecks.

8   In the mid-1970s, Sue was diving for shipwrecks in the Dominican Republic when some friends invited her to go on a day trip to visit an amber mine in the mountains. She decided to go. "A miner showed me an insect preserved in amber," she recalls. "I was fascinated. It looked like it had just been put in the amber, yet it was 23 million years old. That was my introduction to fossils."

(continued)

9   Amber, which is often used to make jewelry, is tree sap that hardened millions of years ago. Sometimes the sap covered insects when it hardened and preserved them perfectly. The trapped insects are highly valued by scientists, museums, and private collectors. Sue Hendrickson became one of the world's leading suppliers of insects encased in amber. She learned how to tell rare from common insects and made repeated trips to the Dominican Republic and Mexico. Just as she had been good at finding lobsters and tropical fish, Sue was good at finding rare insects in the amber. Her most important discoveries were three perfect 23-million-year-old butterflies—half of the world's total collection.

10   The scientists Sue met through the amber trade recognized that she had a sixth sense for finding things, and they encouraged her to join them on digs for dinosaur bones. She spent the next six summers looking for dinosaur bones in the American West, and in 1990, she discovered "Sue."

11   What made that Tyrannosaurus rex so incredible? Sue explains, "Most plant-eating dinosaurs ran in herds, like buffalo. Their bones are easy to find if you know where to look. They look like little bits of popcorn all over the place. The T-rexes, who hunted the plant-eaters, traveled alone or in small groups. You never find them." By 1990, fossil hunters had found only 20 T-rex skeletons, and they were at most only 60 percent complete. "Sue" was 90 percent complete—the only bones missing were part of the left leg and a few bones around the neck—so the skeleton gave scientists their first opportunity to see what the Tyrannosaurus rexes were really like. (For one thing, scientists learned they were huge; Sue is 4 meters tall and 12.8 meters long from her head to the tip of her tail.)

12   When she left South Dakota, Sue gave the T-rex skeleton to one of her colleagues, a fossil hunter named Peter Larson. Peter and Sue had been in love, but the romance had ended; the skeleton, Sue says, was a "breaking up" present. Peter intended to put the skeleton in a small private museum in South Dakota. That was not to be.

13   The rancher who owned the land where "Sue" was found claimed the skeleton belonged to him. Then the U.S. government stepped in and claimed it belonged to the people of the United States. For five years, Peter, the rancher, and the U.S. government fought in court over "Sue." Finally, a judge decided that it belonged to the rancher, who immediately announced he would sell it to the highest bidder. The auction took place in New York City in 1997. The Field Museum of Chicago (with money donated by two corporations, McDonald's and Disney) paid $8.3 million for "Sue"—the highest price ever paid for a fossil.

14   Sue Hendrickson never made a penny from the fossil named after her, and that was all right with her. "It's the thrill of discovery, not the money, that excites me," she says. "Finding is the thing."

15   And why, exactly, is Sue so good at finding things? For one thing, she does her homework. Before she goes on a dig or dive, she reads everything she can; she becomes an expert. But the world is full of experts. Why aren't they making the amazing discoveries that Sue has? Some scientists say Sue Hendrickson has a sixth sense; others call it intuition. Sue just calls her talent "inexplicable." When asked about finding the Tyrannosaurus rex, she says, "I don't think that I found 'Sue.' . . . I think that it chose me. I know it sounds crazy to say a 67-million-year-old dinosaur called to me, but it did. It was like a magnetic pull." ◆

GETTING THE BIG PICTURE

Circle the letter of your answer.

Why is Sue Hendrickson famous in the scientific world?

a. She discovered the only Tyrannosaurus rex skeleton ever found.

b. She has a talent for finding amazing things—a talent that even she cannot explain.

c. She is one of only a few experts on the dinosaur Tyrannosaurus rex.

BUILDING VOCABULARY

◆ RECALLING NEW WORDS

The words below are from the story. Write the correct word or words on the line.

cliff	thrill	inexplicable	vertebrae
rare	donated	a sixth sense	colleagues
herds	fossils		

1. Sue Hendrickson was with a group of scientists who were looking for
   _____; they were especially interested in finding dinosaur
   bones.

2. The people with whom Sue worked went to get a flat tire repaired. While her
   _____ were gone, Sue continued packing.

3. Earlier that summer, Sue had seen a hill with a high, flat side. She decided to
   go back to explore the _____.

4. Because of their size and shape, Sue knew that the three _____
   she discovered were from the backbone of a Tyrannosaurus rex.

5. By 1990, only 20 T-rex skeletons had been found; they are
   _____.

6. Meat-eating dinosaurs hunted alone or in small groups, whereas plant-eating
   dinosaurs hunted in _____.

7. The Field Museum of Chicago was able to pay over $8 million for the
   skeleton because two corporations, McDonald's and Disney,
   _____ money to the museum.

8. Sue Hendrickson has an almost supernatural ability that some people call
   intuition and some call _____.

9. Sue can't explain why she is so good at finding things; she says her talent is
   _____.

10. Sue Hendrickson says that money does not excite her; it is the
    _____ of discovering things that excites her.

◆ UNDERSTANDING SPECIAL EXPRESSIONS

Complete the sentences to show that you understand the meanings of the new words. There may be several correct ways to complete each sentence.

1. *to turn out to be* = to happen in the end (What happened is often not expected.)

Example: We thought the party would be boring, but it turned out to be <u>great.</u>

a. The T-rex skeleton that Sue Hendrickson discovered turned out to be

_____.

b. We thought the car would be cheap, but with air conditioning and anti-lock brakes, it turned out to be _____.

c. They didn't like each other when they first met, but they turned out to be

_____.

2. *to tell* _____ *from* _____ = to see the difference between two things

Example: They are identical twins; even their parents can't tell <u>one</u> from <u>the other.</u>

a. Sue became one of the world's leading suppliers of insects encased in amber, but first she had to learn to tell _____ from

_____.

b. Experts in diamonds can tell _____ from

_____.

c. People who pick and eat wild mushrooms can tell _____ from _____.

DEVELOPING READING SKILLS

◆ UNDERSTANDING THE MAIN IDEAS

Answer each question in a few sentences.

1. Imagine that a friend is looking at the photo on page 78. Your friend points to the skeleton and asks, "What's that?" You say:

_____

_____

_____

2. Next, your friend points to Sue Hendrickson and asks, "Who's she?" You say:

_____

_____

_____

3. Finally, your friend points to the title of the story, "A Sixth Sense," and asks, "What does that mean?" You say:

_____

_____

_____

◆ SCANNING FOR INFORMATION

 Scanning is reading quickly to find specific information. If, for example, you wanted to know the year in which the dinosaur skeleton was sold at auction, you could scan the story for the information. You would move your eyes quickly across the pages, looking for numbers and dates, until you found "1997"—the information you wanted.

Read the list below. Then scan the story to find which six discoveries Sue Hendrickson made. Draw a line through the two discoveries she did not make.

▶ Napoleon's warships

▶ the sunken ship *Titanic*

▶ the most complete T-rex skeleton ever found

▶ Ming Dynasty vases

▶ 23-million-year-old butterflies preserved in amber

▶ Cleopatra's palace

▶ an ancient Indian village in Mesa Verde, Colorado

▶ treasure chests of gold

◆ UNDERSTANDING CHRONOLOGICAL ORDER

Events in a story are usually in chronological order—that is, in the order in which they happened—but sometimes they are not. When they are not, look for phrases that help you understand the chronological order of events (for example, "in 1990" or "when she was 17").

Imagine that Sue Hendrickson took the photos below. Put the photos in chronological order. Write *1* beneath the photo Sue took first, *2* beneath the photo she took second, *3* beneath the photo she took third, and *4* beneath the photo she took last.

a. _____

b. _____

c. _____

d. _____

In the first story, you read that Sue Hendrickson's intuition led her to one of the most important fossil discoveries of the 20th century. Next, you will read about a father and mother whose intuition saved their son's life. The father, a medical doctor, tells the story in his own words.

As you read the story of Jerome Groopman's son, try to visualize the events in the story: the baby crying and lying on his side, the visit to the local pediatrician, and the emergency room. Imagine that the words in the story describe scenes from a private movie that you watch in your mind as you read.

A Parent's Sixth Sense by Jerome Groopman, M.D.

I define a patient's intuition as a powerful and profound sense of his body, both when it is healthy and when something is wrong. Children are often unable to express this intuition about their health. But parents develop a sixth sense about their kids, based on experience and instinct. No physician has such intimate knowledge of your child. When something is wrong, you're usually the first to know. My wife, Pam, and I are both physicians. When our first child, Steven, was 9 months old, he almost died. Our parental intuition helped us save his life.

On the morning of July 4, 1983, during a visit to Pam's parents in Connecticut, we were awakened by Steve's crying. We found him lying on his side, his legs pulled up to his chest, and he was feverish. Something was wrong. A neighbor of Pam's parents called a local pediatrician, who agreed to see us. "Just an intestinal virus; he'll be fine in a day or so," he said. When Pam protested that she knew her baby and something seemed seriously wrong, the pediatrician dismissed her feelings as excess anxiety.

We left Connecticut after we saw the pediatrician and drove up to our home in Boston. As we began to unpack, Steve suddenly took a turn for the worse. We raced him to the Boston Children's Hospital, where he was examined by a young doctor in the emergency room. Pam carefully recited the events of Steven's illness. The doctor ordered X-rays, which revealed what the first doctor had missed: Steve had an intestinal obstruction. As the doctor explained the details of the obstruction, he seemed tired and distracted. "In my experience, there's no need for emergency surgery," he told us.

(continued)

Pam and I sat in stunned silence. We felt—deeply, intuitively—that the advice of this young doctor was incorrect. So we acted—and fortunately, we knew where to turn. I called a physician friend, who contacted a senior surgeon at the hospital. He examined Steve and rushed him to the operating room. The surgery was a success. Our son is now a healthy teenager. But if we had not insisted on a second opinion, it is likely that Steven's bowel would have burst. He would have gone into shock and possibly died.

Physicians who ignore or dismiss a parent's intuition are making a serious mistake. Intuition is a vital element in formulating a diagnosis and treatment. Even if it turns out that your fears were unfounded, it is still helpful to communicate your feelings to the doctor. After listening carefully, he should explain clearly why he disagrees.

Watch out for red flags, such as a physician who dismisses your concerns, won't answer your questions completely or does so in language you can't understand, or becomes irritated or angry when you challenge him. Similarly, a physician who discourages you from getting a second opinion or acts insulted is not the kind of doctor who should be caring for you or your child. Second opinions are essential when your child is facing a severe or life-threatening illness. But they can also be of great benefit in everyday situations when a gut feeling tells you that your doctor's diagnosis may not be correct. ◆

◆ SHARING YOUR TRUE STORIES

Discuss the answers to these questions with your classmates.

1. In his article "A Parent's Sixth Sense," Dr. Groopman gives advice to the parents of sick children—and to all patients. What is Dr. Groopman's advice? What do you think of his suggestions?

2. How do you think most doctors in your country would react if a patient disagreed with the doctor's opinion? How would most doctors in your country react if a patient wanted a second opinion? Have you ever disagreed with a doctor's opinion or gotten a second opinion? Tell the class your story.

3. Have you ever had a "sixth sense" about your health or about a child's health—a "gut feeling" that something was right or wrong? Tell the story to your classmates.

4. Has anyone—a parent or teacher, for example—ever given you advice that you felt—"deeply, intuitively"—was incorrect? What did you do?

Sue Hendrickson's intuition led her to "Sue," one of the most important fossils found in the 20th century, and the intuition of Jerome Groopman and his wife saved their baby's life. What exactly is intuition? Is it a supernatural power that only a few people have? Or is it something that all of us have? In the article below, psychologists explain what they think intuition is and how best to use it.

Before you read, think about the title of the story: "When Not to Use Your Head." To "use your head" is to think about something in a logical and practical way. When could it possibly be a good idea not to think logically?

When Not to Use Your Head

1   At one time or another, probably everyone has had the feeling that something just wasn't right. Perhaps your body sent you a signal: Your neck muscles tightened, or your stomach went into a knot. Maybe a dream seemed to be warning you of danger. Or maybe you were simply becoming increasingly uncomfortable but couldn't explain why. Probably everyone has had the opposite feeling as well: You just knew that something was right and that everything would turn out fine. Some call these feelings hunches, gut feelings, or a sixth sense. Experts call them intuition.

2   Whatever it is called, this knowledge that seems to come out of nowhere has always fascinated people. Now, after decades of study, psychologists believe that they know what intuition is and how to use it.

3   Malcolm Westcott, a professor of psychology in Toronto, Canada, is a leading researcher in the field of intuition. Years ago, Dr. Westcott noticed that some people seem to be exceptionally good at solving problems, and he wondered why. To find out, he did this experiment: He gave people problems to solve but did not give them all the information they needed to solve the problems. Some people simply guessed and were usually wrong. But a small number of people tended to guess the right solutions. What did they do that the others didn't? Apparently they combined the little information Dr. Westcott gave them with bits of knowledge from their own experience to get the right answers.

4   According to Dr. Westcott, this knowledge and experience we carry inside is a key component of intuition. Throughout our lives, we are constantly making complex decisions using the knowledge and experience we have acquired, and we use this knowledge and experience unconsciously—without even knowing we are using it.

5   Consider his example: You hear a loud rumbling noise coming from somewhere beneath your car every time you accelerate. So you take your car in for repair. An inexperienced mechanic might spend hours eliminating each possible cause of the rumble before finding the problem. An experienced mechanic, on the other hand, might take your car out for a five-minute ride, guess what the problem is, and turn out to be right. He could probably not explain how he figured it out so quickly.

6   Herbert Simon, a Nobel Prize winner at Carnegie Mellon University in Pittsburgh, believes that experts often draw on their deep knowledge of problems rather than consciously go through a series of logical steps. "Through experience," Simon says, "an expert's hunches get better and better."

(continued)

7 Many successful people in science, business, the arts, and sports admit that their success is due in part to their intuition. Einstein wrote, "I did not discover the fundamental laws of the universe through my rational mind," and businessman Ray Kroc said he owed his phenomenal success in part to his intuition. In 1961, Kroc wanted to buy a small chain of hamburger-and-milkshake restaurants owned by two brothers named McDonald. The McDonald brothers wanted $2.7 million to close the deal. It was an exorbitant price at that time, and Kroc didn't have that kind of money. He borrowed the money and went ahead anyway because he had "a feeling in his bones." We all know the ending to that story.

8 How can you use your intuition to solve problems, make discoveries, and make better decisions? Writer Paul Bagne interviewed several experts in the field of intuition and asked them for their advice. Here is what the experts say:

9 *1. Do your homework.* A hunch is not just a guess; it has a lot of information behind it. It is important not to confuse fear or other emotions with intuition. Let's say, for example, that you suddenly have an uneasy feeling boarding an airplane. Do you have information and experience that support your uneasy feeling? Is it statistically likely that the plane will crash? Or are you simply afraid of flying? You might be listening to your fear and not to your intuition.

10 *2. Immerse yourself in the problem— then relax.* When trying to make a decision or solve a problem, we sometimes get confused and overwhelmed by all the facts. Experts say that's the time to back off. Go for a walk, work in your garden, visit a friend, or see a movie. It doesn't matter what you do to relax, as long as you enjoy it and are completely occupied by it. Two hundred scientists were asked if a solution had ever just popped into their heads. Nearly 80 percent said yes—usually when they were away from the problem.

11 *3. Trust your experience.* Trust your intuition most in situations where you have a lot of knowledge and experience to draw on; people have the best hunches about what they know the best. And sometimes those hunches seem to go against logic. Stuart Dreyfus, a computer scientist at the University of California in Berkeley, says he would seriously consider a solution that came to him in a flash of intuition, even if the facts suggested another answer. "Usually the brain has done something very sensible when that happens," he says. "It is using previous experience."

12 *4. Double-check your hunch.* Psychologist Jerome Bruner, a professor at New York University, believes that a gut feeling works best as an opening strategy in problem solving. "A gut feeling often gives a sense that something is right or wrong," he says. "But if you stop there, you're nowhere." Many great scientific discoveries, for example, began as hunches, but the hunches were always followed by experiments that proved the hunches were right.

13 People faced with a difficult problem or decision are often advised to "use their heads"—that is, to think about it. But experts say that just thinking is not always enough. Psychologist Westcott says, "Purely rational thinking can lead you only so far. There comes a time when you have to make the leap and trust your intuition." ◆

BUILDING ACADEMIC VOCABULARY

The words below are on the Academic Word List.* Find the words in "When Not to Use Your Head." (The number in parentheses is the number of the paragraph.) If you are not sure what a word means, look it up in your dictionary. Then use the words in the sentences below.

apparently (3)	complex (4)	eliminate (5)	statistically (9)
components (4)	acquired (4)	fundamental (7)	occupy (10)

1. He studied French in school, but he says he _____ most of his knowledge of the language when he lived in Paris.

2. She likes to take a break from work by doing crossword puzzles; she says they _____ her mind.

3. A candle was left burning; _____ that is how the fire started.

4. The soccer team made a _____ mistake when they decided not to start with their best players; they got behind by three goals and were never able to catch up.

5. Every year, more people die in car accidents than in plane crashes. So, it is _____ safer to fly than to drive.

6. Some doctors say the way to lose weight is to _____ fatty and high-carbohydrate foods from your diet.

7. The math problem was so _____ that even the professor had difficulty explaining it.

8. Scientists have identified all the parts of the substance; they say it has hundreds of chemical _____.

DEVELOPING READING SKILLS

◆ UNDERSTANDING THE MAIN IDEAS

Complete each sentence by circling the letter of the best answer.

1. Psychologists say that when we use our intuition, we are using
   a. a supernatural ability that only some of us have.
   b. the knowledge and experience we carry inside.
   c. a key component of our intelligence.

2. Psychologists say that when we use our intuition, we use it
   a. unconsciously—that is, without even knowing we're using it.
   b. foolishly—that is, when we should be using our rational minds.
   c. consciously—that is, by going through a series of logical steps.

*For an explanation and the complete Academic Word List, see page 157.

3. Experiments at a university in Canada showed some people could solve problems even though they didn't have all the information they needed. These people
   a. had a sixth sense for making lucky guesses.
   b. were more intelligent than the people who could not solve the problems.
   c. were using bits of knowledge from their own experience.

4. Intuition can help us
   a. understand dreams and predict the future.
   b. solve problems, make discoveries, and make decisions.
   c. forget our problems and be completely relaxed.

◆ READING ACTIVELY

> Good readers are active readers; they ask questions and make comments as they read. One way to read actively is to write comments and questions in the margins of the book as you read.

Here, for example, is what one student wrote as he read the first paragraph of "When Not to Use Your Head":

That's happened to me.

That, too.

How do experts explain intuition?

> At one time or another, probably everyone has had the feeling that something just wasn't right. Perhaps your body sent you a signal: Your neck muscles tightened, or your stomach went into a knot. Maybe a dream seemed to be warning you of danger. Or maybe you were simply becoming increasingly uncomfortable but couldn't explain why. Probably everyone has had the opposite feeling as well: You just knew that something was right and that everything would turn out fine. Some call these feelings hunches, gut feelings, or a sixth sense. Experts call them intuition.

Reread "When Not to Use Your Head." As you read, write comments and questions in the margins. Do you think asking questions and making comments can help you be a better reader?

◆ CHECKING THE QUALIFICATIONS OF EXPERTS

> When you are reading material that quotes "experts," it is important to check their titles and qualifications. This can help you decide how valuable what they say is. University professors, for example, are usually considered experts, as are people who have had years of experience in their fields.

Check the qualifications of the experts quoted in the article. Match each expert with his title.

Expert	Title
1. Malcolm Westcott, _____	a. psychology professor at New York University
2. Herbert Simon, _____	b. computer scientist at the University of California, Berkeley
3. Stuart Dreyfus, _____	c. Nobel Prize winner, Carnegie Mellon University, Pittsburgh
4. Jerome Bruner, _____	d. psychology professor in Toronto, Canada

◆ **APPLYING INFORMATION**

Imagine that you are in the situations described below. Circle the letter of the answer an expert on intuition would give. Then explain your choice.

1. You are an experienced cook making soup. You're using a recipe you've never tried before. The recipe tells you to put two teaspoons of salt into the soup. That seems like too much. Should you put the two teaspoons of salt into the soup?

   a. Yes   (b.) No

   Experts say, "Trust your intuition most in situations where you have a lot of knowledge and experience." As a cook with experience, I can trust my intuition and use less salt.

2. You have always been a little afraid of high bridges. You are about to drive over a high bridge when suddenly you have a strong feeling that something terrible will happen on the bridge. Should you drive over the bridge?

   a. Yes   b. No

   _____

   _____

   _____

3. You are writing an essay as a homework assignment for a class. You seem to be stuck. For the last half hour you've been staring at the paper and haven't written a single word. Should you get up and do something else for a while?

   a. Yes   b. No

   _____

   _____

   _____

4. You are taking a math test. You suddenly have a hunch that the answer to the problem you're working on is "157." You don't know why the answer is "157"; you just know. Should you write "157" as your answer and go on to the next problem?

a. Yes   b. No

_____

_____

_____

5. Your friend has asked you to color her hair. You have never colored anyone's hair before. The directions on the box of hair color tell you to leave the color on for 20 minutes. You think that can't possibly be enough time. Should you leave the color on her hair a little longer?

a. Yes   b. No

_____

_____

_____

READING A PIE CHART

Bill Taggart is a university professor and a private consultant who helps people use their intuition. Mr. Taggart believes that intuition comes to us in many forms. Read about the forms he says intuition takes:

1. Body	a spontaneous movement of the body (Example: You are walking down the street and you suddenly turn left, even though you didn't plan on turning left.)
2. Sensation or Emotion	Sensations: cold shivers, hair standing on end, hands shaking, muscles becoming tight, stomach going into a knot Emotions: joy, sadness, anger, fear (Emotions and sensations often go together—for example, you might feel afraid and then notice your heart is beating fast.)
3. Thought	an idea that suddenly comes to you
4. Image	a visual picture that suddenly appears in your mind

Mr. Taggart asked over 200 students at a university in the United States to describe intuitive experiences that they have had. Then he asked them what form their intuition had taken. Their responses are recorded in the pie chart on the next page. (It is called a pie chart because it looks like a pie that is cut into pieces.)

What Form Did Your Intuition Take?

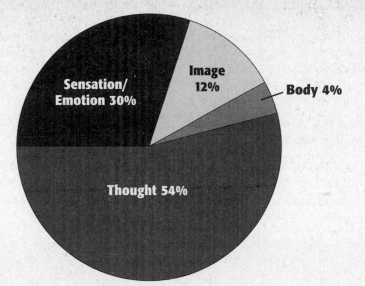

After looking at the pie chart, think about these questions. Discuss your answers with your classmates.

1. What form did intuition take for most of the students?

2. All of the students were studying business. Mr. Taggart thinks that fact may explain why so many of them experienced intuition as a thought. Why do you think business students would be more likely to experience intuition as a thought? Do you think art students or music students would be more likely to experience intuition in a different form?

3. Conduct a survey in your class. Ask your classmates what form their intuition usually takes: body, sensation/emotion, thought, or image. Record the results of your survey in a pie chart. Compare the results of your survey with the results of the survey of the business students.

4. Sit with a partner. Ask your partner if he or she has ever had an experience when intuition came in the form of:

   ▶ a spontaneous body movement

   ▶ a sensation or emotion

   ▶ a sudden thought or idea

   ▶ an image

   Ask your partner to tell you more about his or her experience.

Psychologists say that when we use our intuition, we are using knowledge and experience that we carry inside us. That knowledge and experience is buried in our subconscious, so we cannot access our intuition whenever we want to use it. Craig Karges, the author of the book *Ignite Your Intuition*, believes people can use a pendulum to access their intuition.

A **Read the steps of the pendulum technique. Then follow the steps alone or in a small group.**

1. Make a pendulum. A pendulum is simply a weight hanging from a string. Your pendulum could be a key ring hanging from a string, or it could be a heavy ring hanging from a piece of thread. The weight needs to be suspended by about six inches.

2. Draw a chart like this on a piece of paper:

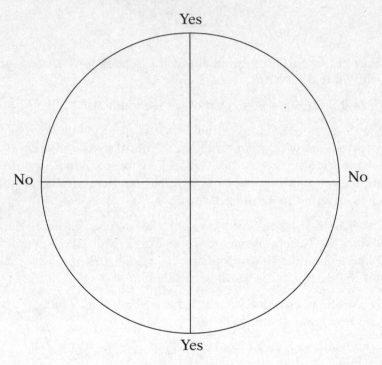

3. Sit at a table and hold the pendulum by the end of its string. Hold the pendulum with one hand and rest your elbow on the table. Hold the pendulum over the chart, above its center and not quite touching the table.

4. Begin by asking a *yes/no* question to which you know the answer, for example, "Is my name _____?" The pendulum should begin to swing slowly back and forth along the *yes* line, perhaps swinging weakly at first and then swinging more strongly. Don't try to get the pendulum to move. Just relax and let it move. Some people will have almost immediate success; others will take longer. Take as much time as you need.

5. Now try asking *yes/no* questions for which you have no sure answer, for example: "Do I need to study more for my math test?" "Should I stay in my present job?" "Is X the right girlfriend for me?" (Most people ask questions about health, finances, and relationships.) If the pendulum swings strongly, you intuitively already knew the answer to your question; you just didn't realize you knew it. If the pendulum swings only weakly or does not swing at all, you probably do not have a strong intuitive answer to your question.

B **Discuss the answers to these questions with your classmates.**

1. Report the results for the pendulum technique. Did the pendulum swing for some people but not for others? Did it swing for people who scored high on the intuition test at the beginning of this unit?

2. Do you think the pendulum technique really helps people get access to their intuition? If so, how does it work? (The answer is on pages 155–156.)

3. Do you think it is important to use your intuition when making an important decision or solving a difficult problem? Why or why not?

4. Would you consider using this technique to help you make a decision or solve a problem? Why or why not?

WRITING

Choose one of the following topics to write about.

1. Read the following statements about intuition. Is there a statement which you believe to be true because of an experience you have had? Write about your experience.

   ▸ Children are very intuitive, especially around age four or five.

   ▸ Many people experience intuition as something physical.

   ▸ Artists and musicians tend to be intuitive.

   ▸ Intuitive people often had imaginary playmates when they were children.

2. Write about a time when you listened to your intuition and were glad you did. Or write about a time when you didn't listen to your intuition and were sorry you didn't.

3. Many successful people say they often use their intuition. Do you know a story about a businessperson, political leader, scientist, or artist—either a historical figure or someone you know—who made a decision, made a discovery, or solved a problem using intuition? Write the story.

4. People faced with a difficult problem or decision might be told, "Use your head." ("Think carefully.") Or they might be told, "Go with your gut." ("Use your intuition.") Which do you think is better advice: "Use your head" or "Go with your gut"? Explain your answer.

Neighborhood Feuds

The theme of this unit is neighborhood feuds—arguments between neighbors that often continue for a long time. You will think about problems that people have with their neighbors and how to solve them.

1. What are some things that make neighbors angry? Work in a group and make a list.

   Example:

   ▸ *Children running around in the apartment upstairs*

   ▸ *Cooking odors that smell bad*

2. Discuss the answers to these questions with your classmates.

   ▸ Have you had an experience with one of the problems on your list? Tell your classmates about it.

   ▸ Do you have a solution to any of the problems? Tell your classmates your solution.

   ▸ Do you think some of the problems you and your classmates listed are universal— that is, common in every part of the world?

In this unit, you will read about the most famous neighborhood feud in U.S. history. Next, you will read the story of a man who remembers how his father, a farmer, avoided having a feud with a neighboring farmer. Finally, you will read about common neighborhood disputes in the United States and how experts recommend resolving them.

1. The Hatfields

2. Roseanna McCoy

PRE-READING

Look at the pictures and read the sentences below. The underlined information is not correct. Replace the underlined words with information that is a more logical guess. Write your answers on the lines. Then share your guesses with the class.

1. Photo 1 was probably taken around <u>1990</u>. _____

2. The people in photo 1 were probably all members of the same <u>club</u>. _____

3. The building behind the people is probably a <u>hospital</u>. _____

4. They probably lived <u>in a big city.</u> _____

5. When you look into the eyes of the woman in photo 2, you can see that she was <u>happy</u>. _____

Now read the story on pages 99–100. How many of your guesses were correct?

Family Feud

1   The most famous family feud in the history of the United States is finally over. The feud between the Hatfield family and the McCoy family, which began in 1878 with an argument over a pig, ended in 2000 with a baseball game.

2   In the late 1800s, the Hatfields and the McCoys lived along a river that ran through the Appalachian Mountains, a mountain range in the eastern United States.  The Hatfields' log house stood on one side of the river, and the McCoys' stood on the opposite side. The river formed the boundary between Kentucky and West Virginia, so the families lived in different states, even though their houses were less than a mile apart. The large McCoy family, led by 53-year-old Randolph McCoy, had a farm on the Kentucky side of the river. The large Hatfield family, led by 40-year-old William Hatfield, had a farm on the West Virginia side. William Hatfield was known for his hot temper; in fact, his nickname was "Devil." Over the years, he had had arguments with neighbors up and down the river.

3   The trouble between the Hatfields and McCoys began in 1878, when Randolph McCoy accused the Hatfields of stealing one of his pigs. This was a serious charge: On a small farm, one pig could make the difference between having enough meat for the winter and going hungry. The Hatfields denied that they had stolen the pig and refused to return it. McCoy took his case to court, which infuriated William Hatfield. After hearing all the evidence, the jury decided, with a vote of seven to five, that the Hatfields were innocent. McCoy was unhappy about the verdict and grumbled about it, but he accepted it. He did not, however, accept what happened next: His daughter Roseanna fell in love with a Hatfield.

4   Roseanna McCoy met William Hatfield's son Johnse (pronounced John-tsee) at a picnic. She was 21 years old and attractive, with dark eyes and dark hair. He was 18 years old, handsome, and fun-loving. They were instantly attracted to each other and spent the day together. At the end of the day, Johnse told Roseanna he loved her and asked her to marry him. She said yes. That evening, instead of going home to her family, Roseanna went home with Johnse to live with the Hatfield family.

5   The next day, Roseanna and Johnse asked Johnse's father for permission to marry. He refused. No son of his, he said, would ever marry a McCoy. Still, Roseanna stayed with the Hatfields. She thought that once William Hatfield got to know her, once he saw how happy she and Johnse were together, he would change his mind. But weeks went by, and he didn't change his mind.

6   Now Roseanna had no place to go. Knowing that she would never be allowed to marry Johnse, she did not want to continue living with the Hatfields. She could not  return to her parents' home because her father was furious with her. Heartbroken, she went to live with an aunt.

7   One day Roseanna overheard her brothers planning an attack on Johnse. In the middle

(continued)

of the night, she sneaked from her aunt's house and rode on horseback to warn Johnse of the danger. Her warning saved Johnse's life, but still William Hatfield did not permit Roseanna and his son to marry.

8   The next conflict between the Hatfields and the McCoys began—once again—at a picnic. The picnic was held not far from the McCoys' farm, on the Kentucky side of the river, and some Hatfields came across the river to attend. Three of Roseanna McCoy's brothers got into an argument with William Hatfield's brother. The argument turned into a fistfight, and the McCoys had weapons—a knife and a gun. William Hatfield's brother was stabbed over a dozen times and then shot. Miraculously, he did not die immediately.

9   A local judge took charge. He arrested the three McCoys and ordered some men to take them to jail. The McCoys never arrived at the jail. When William Hatfield heard about his brother, he organized a group of men. The men captured the McCoys and took them across the river, to the Hatfield side. Hatfield told the three McCoys what their fate would be: "If my brother lives," he said, "you'll live. If he dies, you'll die." William Hatfield's brother died the next day. William Hatfield, with the help of relatives, took the three McCoy sons back to the McCoy side of the river and shot them. The Hatfields left the bodies for the McCoy family to find.

10   After the execution of the three McCoy sons, the feud between the Hatfields and the McCoys escalated into a war between the two families. McCoys came across the river and attacked Hatfields; Hatfields came across the river and attacked McCoys. On New Year's Day, 1888, the Hatfields burned the McCoys' home to the ground, killing two of the McCoy children.

11   The burning of the McCoy house caused panic in Kentucky and West Virginia. Rumors flew that whole communities were at war and

were burning down towns. The governors of both states assured their citizens that soldiers would restore peace if necessary and sent representatives to investigate the situation. All the representatives came back with the same report: Only two families were fighting.

12   The battle between the Hatfields and the McCoys raged until 1889, when the state of Kentucky brought nine Hatfields to trial for the deaths of the McCoy children. One of the Hatfields was hanged, and the other eight were sentenced to life in prison. After that, the fighting between the two families gradually stopped. By 1900, the war was over. It had lasted 12 years, and 12 people had died.

13   Although the Hatfields and McCoys no longer killed one another, hard feelings between the two families continued for generations. Then, in 2000, a man named Bo McCoy, a descendant of Randolph McCoy, decided it was time to officially end the feud. He announced that there would be a reunion of the McCoys and Hatfields in a small town in Kentucky. Over 3,000 people—all descendants of William Hatfield and Randolph McCoy—came to the reunion. For three days, Hatfields and McCoys mingled. They ate together, listened to music, and swapped stories that their grandparents and great-grandparents had told them about the feud.

14   The weekend reunion ended with a friendly game of baseball, the Hatfields against the McCoys. Shouting and cheering, Hatfields and McCoys sat side by side and watched as nine members of the Hatfield family played against nine members of the McCoy family. The McCoys won the baseball game, 15 to 1. The Hatfields were good-natured about their defeat, and not one Hatfield ran to get his shotgun. The feud was over. ◆

GETTING THE BIG PICTURE

Circle the letter of your answer.

The Hatfield-McCoy feud lasted 12 years and left 12 people dead. What is the main reason the feud became so serious and lasted so long?

a. The Hatfields wanted the McCoys' land and animals and would not stop fighting until they had them.

b. The governors of Kentucky and West Virginia could not stop the fighting because whole communities were at war.

c. The problems between the Hatfields and the McCoys escalated; that is, each problem led to a bigger problem.

BUILDING VOCABULARY

◆ RECALLING NEW WORDS

The words below are from the story. Write the correct word on the line.

accused	escalated	refused	verdict
assured	fate	rumors	weapons
denied	mingled		

1. Randolph McCoy said he believed that the Hatfields had taken one of his pigs. He _____ the Hatfield family of stealing.

2. William Hatfield said it was not true that his family had taken the pig. He _____ stealing it.

3. After listening to both sides of the story, the jury made an official decision: Their _____ was that the Hatfields were innocent.

4. When Johnse and Roseanna asked William Hatfield if they could marry, he said that no son of his would ever marry a McCoy. He _____ to give his son permission.

5. The McCoy sons had two _____—a knife and a gun.

6. William Hatfield told the McCoy sons what would happen if his brother died: Their _____ would be the same as his brother's.

7. After the deaths of William Hatfield's brother and the McCoy sons, the fighting between the Hatfields and the McCoys got much worse. It _____ into a war between the two families.

8. One person told another person about the burning of the McCoy house, and then that person told another. Before long, _____ were spreading that entire towns were being burned.

9. The governors told people not to worry: It was not true that whole communities were at war. They _____ people that only two families were fighting.

10. At the reunion, Hatfields and McCoys met and talked with each other. They _____ for three days.

◆ RECOGNIZING RELATED WORDS

"Family Feud" is about a problem between two families. Nine words in the story are related to the word *problem.* In the list below, find the nine words that are related to *problem.* Circle them. The first one is done for you.

history	governor	war	nickname
(argument)	conflict	battle	fistfight
hard feelings	trouble	reunion	feud
picnic	report	fighting	

DEVELOPING READING SKILLS

◆ ORGANIZING INFORMATION BY DRAWING A PICTURE

Historical accounts—like the story of the Hatfields and McCoys—can be difficult to understand because there are many names of people and places. Sometimes it helps to draw a picture as you read. The picture not only helps you understand the story; it also helps you remember it.

The picture below organizes the information in paragraph 2 of "Family Feud." The names of some people and places are missing from the picture. Write each name on the correct line.

Johnse	West Virginia	Randolph McCoy	Appalachian

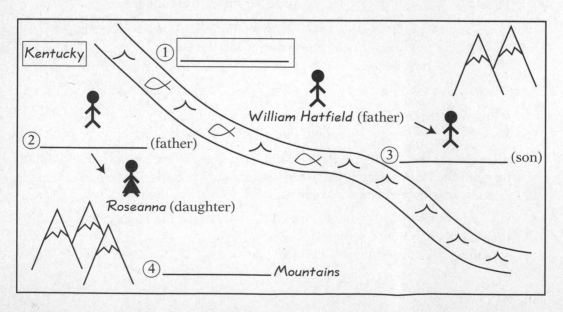

◆ ORGANIZING INFORMATION BY MAKING A TIME LINE

 Another way to organize the information in a historical account is to make a *time line*—a list of events in the order in which they happened. A time line can help you understand the events in a story more clearly.

Below is a time line of the events in "Family Feud." The following sentences are missing from the time line. Complete the time line by writing each sentence in the correct place.

▶ Randolph McCoy's sons get into an argument with William Hatfield's brother, who is stabbed and shot.

▶ The Hatfields burn the McCoys' house down, killing two McCoy children.

▶ Roseanna McCoy and Johnse Hatfield fall in love. William Hatfield does not permit their marriage.

▶ The Hatfield-McCoy war is over. Twelve people are dead.

Hatfield-McCoy Feud Time Line

1878   1. Randolph McCoy accuses the Hatfields of stealing his pig; a jury decides that the Hatfields are innocent.

        2. _____

        _____

        3. Roseanna overhears her brothers' plans to attack Johnse and warns him, saving his life.

        4. _____

        _____

        5. William Hatfield captures the McCoy sons and kills them after his brother dies.

1888   6. _____

        _____

1889   7. Kentucky brings nine Hatfields to trial for the deaths of the McCoy children. One Hatfield is hanged; eight are sentenced to life in prison.

1900   8. _____

        _____

2000   9. Over 3,000 descendants of Randolph McCoy and William Hatfield hold a friendly reunion in Kentucky.

◆ UNDERSTANDING CAUSE AND EFFECT

Complete the sentences. Write your answer on the line. (There may be several correct ways to complete each sentence.)

1. Randolph McCoy took the Hatfields to court because *he believed they had stolen one of his pigs*.

2. Roseanna McCoy didn't want to continue living with the Hatfields because

   _____

   _____.

3. In the middle of the night Roseanna sneaked out of her aunt's house because

   _____

   _____.

4. William Hatfield killed the three McCoy sons because _____

   _____.

5. The governors of West Virginia and Kentucky sent representatives to investigate the conflict between the Hatfields and the McCoys because

   _____

   _____.

6. In 2000, a descendant of Randolph McCoy announced a reunion of the Hatfields and the McCoys because _____

   _____.

A PERSONAL STORY

The Hatfield-McCoy feud began with an argument between two farmers over a stolen pig. Next, you will read a story about another two farmers and their conflict. This true story is told by Ben Logan, the son of one of the farmers. He tells what happened when he and his father discovered a neighbor in one of their cornfields on a hot summer day.

Look at the photo of a field of corn on the next page. When corn is ripe, the corn stalks are higher than a man is tall, so you can't see a man walking in a cornfield; you can see only the stalks moving. Imagine the cornfield in the story, and imagine the stalks moving as the neighbor walks through the field. What do you think the neighbor is doing in the field?

Corn by Ben Logan

One day Father was fixing a fence way out at the northwest corner of the farm. I took him a bucket of lemonade. As I walked along the dusty road, I saw an old Ford hidden in the brush of some woods that were across the road from our cornfield. I told Father about the car when I gave him the lemonade. He thought about it for a minute, then propped up his shovel against a tree. "You show me."

We walked along the fence and crossed the road into the woods. Father wouldn't let me talk. We moved carefully through the bright red of the sumacs. I showed him the car. He went up to it, reached in, and found some empty burlap bags—gunny sacks, we called them. He looked across the road at our cornfield. It was early corn, already turning brown and rattling in the wind. There was yellow showing at the ends of some of the ears.

Father crossed the road. I started after him. I was pretty sure whose car it was—the new neighbor, the one people said had killed his own brother.

Father saw me following and shooed me back. He smiled. "It's all right. There won't be any trouble. It takes two to make trouble."

He moved into the cornfield, walking very quietly. I followed anyway. In a minute he found the man pulling off ears of corn, stuffing them into a bag. Father pulled an ear off a stalk, walked up, and tossed it into the bag. The man jumped, and started to run. Father stepped in front of him. The man stood there and Father went on snapping ears of corn and tossing them into the bag.

"You should have told me you needed corn. We've got some of last year's in the crib you could borrow. That'd be better. Some of this isn't ripe yet."

The man didn't say a word. Father slowly filled the bag. "That enough for now?"

The man nodded.

"Let me carry it for you." Father swung the bag to his shoulder and carried it to the car. The man followed.

"There," Father said. "I'll drop off a couple more bags tomorrow. Let me know if you need more. No hurry about paying it back. You'll be harvesting this fall, I suppose."

The man nodded.

"Why not wait until then," Father said. He put his hand on my shoulder. "Well, son. Let's get back to that fence."

The man took a step toward us. Father stuck out his hand. The man nodded again and took the hand.

At harvest time that fall, the man drove into our barnyard and unloaded half a dozen sacks of corn into the crib. ◆

Discuss the answers to these questions with your classmates.

1. Ben Logan's story "Corn" is from his book *The Land Remembers*. The book is a memoir—a collection of memories. Ben Logan writes his memories of growing up on a farm in Wisconsin in the 1930s. What is the difference between a memoir and an autobiography?

2. Ben Logan was riding the subway in New York City when the young woman sitting next to him suddenly laughed. He turned and saw she was reading his book. "Good book?" he asked her. "Yes," she said, still laughing. "A very good book." Why do you think the New Yorker was reading a book about a family who lived on a Wisconsin farm in the 1930s? Why do people read memoirs? Have you ever read a memoir, either in English or in your native language? Why did you read it?

3. What do you think about the way Ben Logan's father solved the problem with his neighbor? Do you think the Hatfields could have solved their problem with the McCoys in the same way? Would you try Mr. Logan's solution if a neighbor were stealing from you?

4. When Ben Logan's father went into the cornfield to investigate, he assured his son, "It's all right. There won't be any trouble. It takes two to make trouble." What does that mean: "It takes two to make trouble"? Is that true?

NEWS AND VIEWS

When he believed that one of the Hatfields stole his pig, Randolph McCoy tried to resolve the conflict by going to court. Ben Logan's father used a very different tactic when he discovered a neighbor stealing his corn: He gave his neighbor the corn.

What is the best way to resolve conflicts between neighbors? The author of the following article has some suggestions.

Preview the article before you read it; that is, read short parts before you read the whole text. Preview this way:

▶ Read the title and subheadings.

▶ Read the first paragraph.

▶ Read the first sentence of every paragraph.

▶ Read the last paragraph.

As you read, think about this: Did previewing the article make it easier for you to understand it?

Neighborhood Feuds by Mark Stuart Gill

1   Across the United States, disputes between neighbors are becoming common. The most common conflicts fall into three categories: excessive noise; damage caused by children and pets; and trees (for instance, a neighbor's maple tree blocking your view).

2   As trivial as these irritations may seem, when they occur repeatedly they can start all-out war. For instance, in one California town, a man was so enraged by persistent barking from his neighbor's dog that he taped the pet's mouth shut. The dog died, and the man now faces criminal charges for animal cruelty. In a Connecticut neighborhood, when a family refused to trim their messy weeping-willow tree, someone drilled holes in the tree's trunk and poisoned it.

3   When a neighbor problem arises, people usually try to avoid the neighbor. They are afraid they will insult or offend the neighbor if they talk about the problem. That is probably not the best tactic; avoiding a problem neighbor makes people feel helpless, like there is no solution.

4   Lawsuits are also usually a poor solution. A lawyer who specializes in neighbor problems says, "Courts hate neighbor lawsuits. Lawsuits often just mask the real problems between neighbors. So, even after the lawsuit is over, the neighbors find something else to fight about."

What You Can Do

5   So, if avoiding a problem neighbor isn't an effective solution, and neither is filing a lawsuit, how do you handle a dispute with a neighbor? Experts say to handle it yourself.

6   To begin with, know your rights. When a neighbor does something extremely unreasonable, he or she has probably broken a "nuisance law." These laws vary from community to community, but they are often very detailed. For instance in Farmington, New Mexico, music played on private property is not allowed to exceed fifty decibels at night. Check the local laws at your town clerk's office or the public library. If you have legal grounds to complain, show your neighbor a copy of the law.

7   Unfortunately, being on the right side of the law isn't always enough. To prevent the problem from turning into a battle, keep in mind that different types of neighbor problems call for different strategies:

8   *Noise.* Experts in neighborhood mediation advise people to remember that noise is subjective. The neighbor might not even realize he or she is creating a problem. You might think that the rock 'n roll band next door is making noise, but they think they are making important music. When you approach a neighbor about a noise problem, don't criticize the neighbor's behavior; that might only make the neighbor angry. Instead, tell your neighbor how the sound is affecting you. For example, instead of saying, "Your guitars are too loud," say, "Your guitars are keeping me and my family awake at night."

9   *Kids and pets.* Children and domestic animals have the greatest potential to tear a neighborhood apart. Take the case of Michael Rubin, who was involved in one of the most bitter neighbor lawsuits in the United States.

10   One day Rubin came home and decided to take a nap. Outside his bedroom window, the boy next door was playing basketball. Rubin recalls, "I asked the boy to stop playing basketball. He stopped, but then came out with his father and started playing again." Rubin grabbed a garden hose and soaked the boy and his father.

11   The neighbors sued Rubin. They claimed that his spraying them with water caused such emotional distress, they had to go into therapy, and they wanted him to pay for it. Rubin countersued his neighbors.

(continued)

12   What can neighbors do to avoid this legal and emotional war? In a case involving a neighbor's child, it pays to be especially careful. People can be hypersensitive and defensive about their kids. Instead of reacting in the heat of the moment, take some time to think about how you want to solve the problem. Then calmly approach your neighbors.

13   *Trees.* Trees are one of the trickiest neighbor problems to resolve. That's because they serve so many vital purposes to a homeowner. They may be used for privacy, shade, fences, property line markers or even food. So, in the case of a problem tree, be prepared to compromise.

14   That's something Amy King wishes she had done. Every autumn, Amy collected the apples that dropped from her neighbor's trees into her yard, to make cider. There was no fence between the yards, so Amy collected only the apples that she was sure had fallen on her side of the property line. Last year, her neighbor gave her a bill. "The trees belong to me," he said. "If you want to use my apples, you have to pay for them."

15   Furious, Amy trimmed the apple-tree branches that hung over her property line. The neighbor fought back: He hired a tree consultant who claimed the trees were traumatized, and he wanted payment for the damage.

16   She could have avoided these troubles by compromising with her neighbor. For instance, she might have suggested that she'd be willing to allow the branches to hang over her property—and not collect the apples—if her neighbor would remove the apples that fell into her yard.

Declaring a Truce

17   Unfortunately, some neighbors are not willing to be reasonable. Instead, they become threatening, even violent.

18   In such cases, the ideal solution may be to bring in a neutral third party to mediate. Neighbor mediation is remarkably successful. The American Bar Association reports that, on average, over 250,000 neighbors a year try mediation to resolve disputes. Of those, 80 percent reach a satisfactory written agreement.

19   In short, if you are having a dispute with your neighbor, don't avoid the neighbor and don't file a lawsuit. It is unlikely that either of those tactics will work. Try handling the problem yourself, remembering to use these strategies: Don't criticize your neighbor's behavior; instead, explain how the behavior is affecting you. Rather than react in the heat of the moment, think about what you want to say and then say it calmly. Be ready to compromise. If your neighbors are breaking the law, show them a copy of the law. If these strategies don't work, try mediation—a tactic that will work almost 80 percent of the time. ◆

BUILDING VOCABULARY

◆ UNDERSTANDING ACADEMIC VOCABULARY

The words below are on the Academic Word List.* Find the words in "Neighborhood Feuds." (The number in parentheses is the number of the paragraph.) If you are not sure what a word means, look it up in your dictionary. Then use the words in the sentences below.

categories (1)	exceeding (6)	potential (9)	resolve (13)
persistent (2)	strategy (7)	involved in (9)	neutral (18)
vary (6)	domestic (9)		

1. The tickets _____ in price: Seats near the stage cost $50, but balcony seats cost only $15.

2. She's been coughing since she caught a cold a month ago. Today she's going to the doctor for medicine for her _____ cough.

3. Parking spaces at the university fall into three _____: parking for visitors; parking for staff and faculty; and parking for students who commute from home to campus.

4. She has a ten-page paper due in three weeks. She plans to do research the first week, write an outline and rough draft the second week, and type the final draft the third week. That's her _____ for getting the paper finished on time.

5. Switzerland refuses to take sides in international conflicts and for centuries has remained _____ in wartime.

6. He always seems to be unhappy with the grades he gets; right now, he is _____ a dispute with his English professor over the grade he got on his essay.

7. Businesses are complaining that cooking odors from a neighborhood restaurant are coming into their shops. The restaurant hopes to _____ the dispute, perhaps by installing a large fan.

8. Doctors are warning people that some weight-loss pills can possibly cause health problems; some pills even have the _____ for causing heart attacks.

9. She was driving 70 miles per hour in a 55-mile-per-hour zone. She got a ticket for _____ the speed limit.

10. Police officers are careful when trying to resolve a conflict between a husband and wife in their home; _____ arguments can sometimes become violent.

*For an explanation and the complete Academic Word List, see page 157.

◆ UNDERSTANDING LEGAL TERMS

Imagine that you are having a problem with your neighbor. Read about the situation. Then match each boldfaced legal term with the words or phrases that have the same meaning. Write the letter of your answer on the line.

Your neighbor Joe has piles of trash in his yard. You've asked him to remove the trash and he has refused. Joe says there's nothing you can do about the piles of trash. He says you have no legal **(a) grounds** to complain. But you know **(b) your rights.** You decide to **(c) file a lawsuit.** You claim in your lawsuit that your house has lost value because of Joe's trash and you want him to remove the trash.

When Joe learns that you have filed a lawsuit against him, he is upset. He says he is so upset, he can't eat or sleep. He **(d) countersues:** He wants you to pay him money for upsetting him. You try to resolve your dispute with Joe by asking a **(e) third party** to help you and Joe talk about your problem. But Joe does not agree to the mediation.

In the middle of the night you go into Joe's yard and take the trash. When Joe sees that his trash is gone, he calls the police. You admit to the police that you are the one who took the trash. Now the police say you **(f) face criminal charges**!

_____ 1. responds to your lawsuit against him by suing you

_____ 2. might be guilty of a crime, and you will have to go through a legal process

_____ 3. go to court and officially record your complaint against Joe

_____ 4. neutral person—someone who is not a friend of either you or Joe

_____ 5. what you are allowed to do

_____ 6. reasons

DEVELOPING READING SKILLS

◆ UNDERSTANDING THE MAIN IDEAS

Use the phrases and words below to complete sentences 1–4. Write your answers on the lines.

> explain to your neighbor how the behavior is affecting you
>
> bring in a neutral third party to mediate
>
> ~~avoid the neighbor~~
>
> check to see if your neighbor has broken a law
>
> take some time to cool off; then calmly approach your neighbor
>
> file a lawsuit
>
> compromise

1. If you have a problem with a neighbor, you should not
   a. *avoid the neighbor.*

   b. _____

2. If a neighbor does something extremely unreasonable, the first thing you

   should do is _____

3. Three strategies that usually work for solving neighbor problems are

   a. _____

   b. _____

   c. _____

4. If the three strategies above do not work, and your neighbor becomes

   threatening or violent, then the ideal solution may be to _____

   _____

◆ **APPLYING INFORMATION**

Do the following activities with your classmates.

1. Read the list of neighbor problems you and your classmates made at the
   beginning of this unit on page 97. If you would like to add problems to the
   list, do so. Think about the strategies for resolving neighbor disputes
   suggested in the article "Neighborhood Feuds," as well as the solutions you
   and your classmates suggested at the beginning of this unit.

2. With a partner, choose one of the problems on the list. Then role-play with
   your partner. One person plays the part of the neighbor causing the problem,
   and the other person plays the part of the neighbor trying to find a solution.
   (A third classmate can be a mediator—a neutral third party who tries to help
   you resolve your dispute.)

3. Role-play your conversation with your "neighbor" in front of the class.

READING A LIST

A A mediator who helps settle disputes in Ohio made a list of the top causes of neighborhood feuds there. The most common problems are at the top of the list and the least common problems are at the bottom. Read the list.

Top Seven Causes of Neighborhood Feuds in Ohio, U.S.A.

1. **Noise**
   dogs barking, loud music, noisy children

2. **Control of pets**
   pets coming into neighbor's yard

3. **Condition of yard**
   lawn not mowed, litter, hedges not trimmed

4. **Control of children**
   children coming into neighbor's yard

5. **Parking**
   neighbors and their guests parking in front of others' homes

6. **Trees and hedges**
   tree hanging over neighbor's roof; tree blocking view;
   tree creating a mess; hedge blocking visibility,
   making it dangerous for neighbor to pull out of driveway

7. **Rumors and gossip**
   people spreading rumors that a neighbor
   got fired from his job, drinks too much,
   cheats on his wife, etc.

   Rumors and gossip are sometimes the real reasons behind complaints 1–6.

B 1. **Make a list of problems that are the top causes of neighborhood conflicts in your country. Give an example of each problem.**

Example:

▶ *Trash (leaving trash in the hallway)*

2. **Compare your list with the list made by a classmate from a different country. Are there any problems that are common in your partner's country but not in yours?**

DISCUSSION

A Below are descriptions of actual neighborhood feuds. Read about the feuds. Then, in a small group, decide on a fair way to resolve each dispute. Tell the group how the dispute would be resolved in your country.

1. A man in southern Germany likes to grill Bratwurst (sausages that are popular in Germany) in his yard. His neighbor doesn't like the smoke.

2. A church in Washington, D.C., has a large kitchen and wants to give free meals to the poor and homeless. Neighbors do not want the "soup kitchen" to open. They are worried that the people coming for free meals will bring more crime into the area.

3. A California woman has piles of trash in her yard. She has three old cars, a rusted washer and dryer, several bookcases, a sofa, old tires, shopping carts, an old table and chairs, and chunks of concrete in front of her house. The neighbors are tired of looking at the junk, and the houses nearest the woman's house have lost value.

4. A billionaire in the state of Washington is building a "monster house"—a house ten times bigger than the other houses in the neighborhood. The mansion will be under construction for two years. Neighbors are complaining that building the house has turned their neighborhood into a construction zone, with dump trucks, bulldozers, and work crews arriving at 6 A.M. One neighbor is suing the billionaire for $1 million. "The noise is unbearable," she says.

5. A parrot named Bubba is causing trouble in a Florida neighborhood. His owner keeps the parrot on her screened-in balcony. Neighbors claim the parrot's loud screeches bother them. They also claim that the parrot uses bad words. One neighbor says the parrot told her, "Shut up, you #%@*&!" Bubba's owner says the parrot is learning the bad words not from her, but from the neighbors. She refuses to bring the parrot inside.

B Share your group's ideas for resolving the disputes with the class. Then look on page 156 to see how the disputes were actually resolved.

WRITING

Choose one of the following topics to write about.

1. Describe a neighbor that you have or once had.

2. Have you ever had a dispute with a neighbor? What was the dispute about? How was the dispute resolved?

3. Roseanna McCoy was not allowed to marry Johnse Hatfield because their fathers hated one another. Do you have a story in your own family about someone who was not permitted to marry the person he or she loved? Tell the story in writing.

4. A line in a poem by Robert Frost is "Good fences make good neighbors." What do you think the line means? Do you think it is true?

5. The author of "Neighborhood Feuds" gives these suggestions for resolving conflicts between neighbors:

   ▶ Don't criticize your neighbor's behavior; instead, explain how the behavior is affecting you.

   ▶ Rather than react in the heat of the moment, think about what you want to say and then say it calmly.

   ▶ Be ready to compromise.

   These strategies seem to work in the United States. Would they work just as well in your country? Explain why they would or wouldn't.

The Stock Market

In this unit, you will read about the stock market. A stock is a part of a company that people can buy. The "stock market" refers to the value of stocks and the business of buying and selling them.

1. Look at the list below. It is similar to those found in newspapers in many parts of the world. It is a list of stock prices. Do you know what the numbers and letters in the list mean? Take a guess. Then look on page 156 to see if your guesses were right.

NYSE

— A —

52-week High	Low	Stock	Div	PE	Last	Change
17.45	6.96	AAR	.10	...	13.00	−.15
18.95	6.10	ABB Ltd	...	...	8.36	−.55
20.44	14.20	ABN Amro	.80e	...	20.14	−.18
26.08	24.26	ABN pfA	1.88	...	25.04	+.04
25.65	24.00	ABN pfB	1.78	...	24.64	+.06
44.98	18.10	ACE Ltd	.60f	...	43.82	+.01
9.00	7.25	ACM Inco	.84	...	7.99	+.03
8.32	6.30	ACMMD	.81	...	7.20	+.03
5.05	3.80	ACM MI	.51	...	4.46	+.01

52-week High	Low	Stock	Div	PE	Last	Change
57.05	31.70	AffCmpS s		35	51.20	−1.50
74.50	47.30	AffMgrs		31	67.70	−.96
9.50	2.50	Agere	...	...	3.95	+.28
41.18	18.00	Agilent	...	...	33.75	−1.25
14.48	6.80	Agnico g	.02	...	u14.42	+.19
13.18	8.72	Agrium g	.11	...	10.04	−.10
31.95	23.03	Ahold	.53e	...	24.73	−.26
53.52	32.25	Air Prod	.80	24	49.12	−1.08
20.90	7.00	Airborne	.16	...	18.32	−.12
20.74	8.40	Airgas		33	17.99	−.61
12.25	2.60	AirTran	...	...	6.25	+.05
26.25	23.55	AlaPC pfQ	1.84	...	24.75	−.12
20.00	3.00	Alamosa	...	...	5.43	−.57
33.90	17.40	AlskAir		...	31.00	−.26
30.65	14.18	Albnyln	.20	26	27.00	+.58

52-week High	Low	Stock	Div	PE	Last	Change
25.35	18.05	Amerigas	2.20	29	22.63	+.14
72.30	50.00	AmerisBrg	.10	32	u72.76	+.46
40.20	21.37	Ametek	.24	18	36.26	−.84
57.99	32.00	Amphenol		27	45.65	−1.29
22.92	15.61	AmSouth	.88	15	22.45	−.30
69.39	43.00	Anadrk	.30	16	54.45	−.55
53.30	29.00	AnalogDev		43	41.05	−.45
26.07	15.20	Anglogld	.65e	...	25.43	+.33
52.97	38.74	Anheusr	.72	28	52.63	+.43
32.00	22.40	Anixter		40	30.29	−.33
47.77	21.10	AnnTayl		46	45.82	−.92
17.62	10.61	Annaly	2.52f	8	16.65	...
37.25	15.55	AnnuityLf	.20	...	20.03	−.65
23.40	19.25	Anteon n		...	u23.00	...

2. Which of the words below do you think you will probably find in this unit? Circle them.

company	investor	pizza	stockbroker
health	library	product	stockholder
investment strategy	money manager	profit	stock portfolio

In this unit, you will read about a woman who made a lot of money—$22 million, to be exact. Next you will read about a man who had the opposite experience: He lost all his money. Finally, you will read about a group of women who followed some simple rules for investing in the stock market. Did the women make money? Read their story to find out.

PRE-READING

Look at the photo and read the title of the story on the next page. Think about these questions and discuss your answers with your classmates.

▶ The woman in the photo, Anne Scheiber, invested her small savings in the stock market and made a fortune. Do you think she was particularly smart? Or particularly lucky?

▶ Do you think anyone can do what Anne Scheiber did?

A Smart Investor

1   While Anne Scheiber was alive, no one paid much attention to her. She had no husband, no friends, and hardly any contact with her four brothers and four sisters. She rarely left her small apartment, and when she did go out, she was almost invisible—a short, thin woman dressed entirely in black. But when she died at age 101, Anne Scheiber suddenly became famous. It turned out that Miss Scheiber was rich, and she left her fortune—$22 million—to Yeshiva University in New York City, a school she had never attended and never even visited.

2   The story of how Anne Scheiber made her fortune is as fascinating as why she gave it all away. Anne's father died when she was a child, leaving her mother with nine children to support. Anne's mother managed to feed and clothe her family, but money was tight. Whenever the family had any extra money, it went to educate the four sons; the five daughters were on their own.

3   Anne started working as a bookkeeper when she was 15 and went to school at night, eventually graduating from college with a law degree. She decided not to practice law, however. Instead, she went to work for the Internal Revenue Service (the I.R.S.) in Washington, D.C., as a tax auditor. Her job was to examine income tax returns and look for errors. Anne was a diligent employee who excelled at her work. Although she was only five feet tall and weighed 100 pounds, her favorite technique was to scare people when she thought they were cheating on their taxes. "These are not the correct figures," she would tell them. "Come back tomorrow with the real figures." She was described as "a terror." Yet, in the 23 years that Anne worked for the I.R.S., she was never promoted, and she got only small pay raises.

4   Anne learned two lessons in her years of working at the I.R.S. First, she concluded that women had little chance of succeeding, no matter how hard they worked. Second, from examining thousands of income tax records she learned that the surest way to get rich in the United States was to invest in stocks. Anne Scheiber felt that the I.R.S. had treated her unfairly, and she wanted revenge. She decided to get even by getting rich. Even though she was earning very little money, she saved as much as she could; some years, she saved 80 percent of her salary. Then she used her savings to invest in the stock market. By 1936, she had $21,000 invested in stocks. But it wasn't until 1944, when Anne retired at age 50, that she became a full-time investor.

5   Anne retired from the I.R.S. with a small pension and a savings account of $5,000 in cash. She moved to New York City, the financial center of the United States, and rented a small apartment. Then she began to study the stock market in the same diligent way she had studied income tax returns. She decided to invest first in industries she knew something about. She loved Hollywood movies, so she investigated the studios. Which studios were the most successful? Using information she got from newspapers at the public library, she kept track of attendance records for recent movies. Two studios—Paramount and Universal—seemed to produce the most popular movies. She bought stock in both studios. She bought stock in a broadcasting company called Capital Cities, which later became Disney Corporation. She bought stock in Coca-Cola and later in Pepsi-Cola. She bought stock in drug companies like Bristol-Myers Squibb and Schering-Plough.

(continued)

6   Anne's investment strategy was simple. First, she didn't put all her eggs in one basket—she ultimately invested in 100 companies, not just in one or two. Second, she invested only in leading companies whose products she understood. Third, she almost never sold stocks. When the value of her stocks fell, she hung on to them, convinced they would be worth something in the long run.

7   By 1970, Anne Scheiber had turned her small savings into a stock portfolio worth millions, but she certainly didn't live like a millionaire. Her home was the same tiny apartment she rented when she moved to New York, furnished with the same tables, chairs, and lamps she had bought in 1944. Paint was peeling off the walls, and dust covered the bookcases. She often skipped meals to save money on food, and she walked everywhere to save money on bus fare, even when it rained. She never bought a newspaper—instead, she walked to the library and read the *Wall Street Journal* there—and she rarely bought new clothes. Everywhere she went, she wore the same cheap black coat—fall, winter, and spring. (Once, a niece bought her a new black coat, and when Anne found out that it had cost $150, she refused to wear it.) Saving and investing money was her obsession. Every penny Anne had, she used to buy stocks.

8   The sacrifices Anne made to invest in the stock market were not only material; there were social sacrifices, too. Her entire world was her investments. She shut out her family and friends, and she never had a sweetheart. The only social events Anne attended were stockholders' meetings of the companies whose stock she owned. Whenever a stockholders' meeting was in New York City, Anne Scheiber was there. She would go directly to the CEO of the company and demand answers to her questions, just as she had when she was an auditor at the I.R.S. In the last years of her life, Anne left her apartment only to visit her lawyer, her stockbroker, or to see her stock certificates, which were kept in a vault in her stockbroker's offices near Wall Street. She would walk to the offices, look over her stock certificates, and then walk back to her apartment. "She did that a lot," her stockbroker says.

9   When Anne Scheiber died in 1995 at the age of 101, she had $22 million in stocks. In her will, she left $50,000 to the niece who had bought her the black coat, and she gave the rest of the money to Yeshiva University. She specified that the money was to be used for scholarships and loans for women only. In the end, Anne Scheiber did indeed get even: There is no tax on money given to schools, so not one penny of Anne's fortune went to her former employer, the I.R.S.

10   When news of Anne Scheiber's $22 million gift spread, she suddenly got the attention she had never had while she was alive. People poured over her stock portfolio, curious to see which stocks had made her a multimillionaire. Newspapers called her "amazing," "wise," and "brilliant." But money managers pointed out that one didn't have to be a genius to accomplish what Anne Scheiber did. Anne Scheiber began buying stocks as early as 1936 and died in 1995. So, she owned some stocks for over 50 years. According to money managers, that investment strategy—buying stock and holding onto it for a long time—has always been successful. Yes, they said, Anne Scheiber was smart. But perhaps the smartest thing she did was live to be 101. ◆

GETTING THE BIG PICTURE

What were the reasons for Anne Scheiber's success in the stock market?
Check (✓) two reasons.

❏ When her father died, she received a small fortune and invested it in the stock market.

❏ She used wise investment strategies: investing in more than one company, investing only in leading companies, and not selling stocks.

❏ Friends who were the CEOs of big companies told her which stocks to buy.

❏ She owned some stocks for over 50 years.

BUILDING VOCABULARY

◆ RECALLING NEW WORDS

Which words have the same meaning as the italicized words from the story?
Circle the letter of the correct answer.

1. Anne Scheiber saw her family only once or twice a year. She had *hardly any* contact with them.
   a. almost no
   b. regular

2. After she died, Anne Scheiber got the attention she never had while she was alive. People found her story *fascinating*.
   a. very interesting
   b. difficult to believe

3. The Scheiber family never went on vacations, never ate at restaurants, and never owned a new car. *Money was always tight*.
   a. There was not enough money.
   b. All their money was in the bank.

4. Anne worked during the day and went to classes only at night, so it took her years to finish school. *Eventually,* she graduated from college with a degree in law.
   a. after a lot of hard work
   b. after a long time

5. If Anne thought people were not being honest, she would say, "These are not the correct figures. Come back tomorrow with the real figures!" Her *technique* usually worked.
   a. way of doing something
   b. angry words

6. In the 23 years that Anne worked at the I.R.S., she always had the same job. She was never *promoted*.
   a. told she was doing a good job
   b. given a more important, higher-paying job

7. Anne believed that the I.R.S. had been unfair to her. She wanted to *get even*.
   a. hurt the I.R.S. as much as the I.R.S. had hurt her
   b. ask the I.R.S. for a big pay raise and a promotion

8. Anne didn't worry when the price of her stocks fell because she believed that they would make money in the future. She was sure they would be worth something *in the long run*.
   a. if she sold them
   b. at a later time

9. Anne never bought new clothes, new furniture, or even a newspaper. She made a lot of *sacrifices* to save money.
   a. things of poor quality that you get free or very cheaply
   b. the decision not to have valuable things in order to get something that is more important to you

10. Anne could think of nothing else but saving and investing money. It was her *obsession*.
    a. an extreme, unhealthy interest in something
    b. something you do in your free time because you find it enjoyable

11. At stockholders' meetings, Anne would ask the *CEO* questions about the company.
    a. the chief executive officer, the person with the most authority in a company
    b. the company export official, the person in charge of sales to foreign countries

12. When Anne wrote her will, she knew exactly who she wanted to get her money. She *specified* that the money was for female students only.
    a. hoped it would be possible
    b. stated in an exact and detailed way

◆ USING NEW WORDS

Complete the sentences with examples from your own life. In small groups, take turns reading your sentences aloud. Ask your classmates questions about their sentences.

1. I have hardly any _____.

2. I think it's fascinating to learn about _____.

3. When money is tight, I don't _____.

4. Eventually I hope to _____.

5. I know a good technique for _____.

6. I would try to get even if someone _____.

7. I would make sacrifices in order to _____.

8. If I wrote my will, I would specify that _____.

DEVELOPING READING SKILLS

◆ UNDERSTANDING CAUSE AND EFFECT

Complete the sentences. Write your answer on the line. The first one is done for you.

1. When Anne Scheiber died, she suddenly became famous because *she gave her fortune of $22 million to a university*_____.

2. Money was always tight for the Scheiber family because _____
   _____.

3. Anne wanted to get even with her employer, the I.R.S., because _____
   _____.

4. Anne decided to invest her money in the stock market because _____
   _____.

5. Anne never bought new furniture, clothes, or even a newspaper because _____
   _____.

6. No male students at Yeshiva University received any money from Anne
   Scheiber because _____.

7. Yeshiva University didn't pay tax on the $22 million they received from Anne
   Scheiber because _____
   _____.

8. Money managers said that Anne Scheiber made a fortune in the stock market
   mainly because _____
   _____.

♦ UNDERSTANDING MAIN IDEAS AND SUPPORTING DETAILS

The ability to understand the main ideas and the details that support them is an important reading skill.

Main ideas are important facts and events; without them, a story doesn't make sense. *Supporting details* often make a story more interesting, but the story would still make sense without them. For example, the fact that Anne Scheiber had a law degree is not a main idea of the story; the story would still make sense without that information.

Check (✓) the six facts that give you the main ideas of Anne Scheiber's story.

Anne Scheiber

❑ had four sisters and four brothers.

❑ dressed entirely in black.

❑ worked for the I.R.S as a tax auditor.

❑ was five feet tall and weighed 100 pounds.

❑ believed that the I.R.S. was unfair to her.

❑ wanted to get even with the I.R.S. by getting rich.

❑ loved Hollywood movies.

❑ made great sacrifices so that she could invest every penny she had in the stock market.

❑ read the *Wall Street Journal* at the library.

❑ often walked to her stockbroker's offices to look at her stock certificates.

❑ had a fortune of $22 million when she died.

❑ gave almost all her money to a university, specifying it was for women only.

♦ EXPANDING ON THE STORY

Imagine this: After Anne Scheiber died, a newspaper reporter interviewed people who knew her. The reporter asked them the questions below. What do you imagine they might have said?

Role-play in small groups. One student plays the role of the reporter. The other students play the parts of the people below. Conduct the interviews "live" in class. The first one is done for you.

Reporter: Did you know Anne Scheiber well?

Neighbor: *"I hardly ever saw her. She stayed in her apartment most of the time and didn't socialize with the neighbors. I'd see her come and go once in a while, but I never talked to her. "*

Reporter: I understand that you once gave your aunt a gift that she returned. Could you tell us about that?

Niece: _____

_____

Reporter:	Is it true that Anne Scheiber attended stockholders' meetings? What did she do there?
CEO:	_____
	_____
Reporter:	What kind of worker was Anne Scheiber? Do you think she was happy at the I.R.S.?
I.R.S. co-worker:	_____
	_____
Reporter:	Could you briefly describe Ms. Scheiber's investment strategies?
Anne's stockbroker:	_____
	_____

A PERSONAL STORY

Anne Scheiber made $22 million by investing in the stock market. Next, you will read about an investor who bought stocks but did not have the success that Anne Scheiber did.

As you read the article below, do not look up any words in your dictionary. Instead, cross out (X) every word or expression that you don't know. Then read the article again, without reading the words you crossed out. If you can briefly explain how Walter Kirn lost money in the stock market, then you have understood the main idea of this reading, even though you may not know the meaning of every word.

How I Lost Money in the Bull Market[1] by Walter Kirn

I was born a United States citizen, but last year I became a true American. I started buying stocks.

And selling them, which was the problem. In 1995—a year when anybody could have made money on Wall Street—I lost money. Not a lot, but more than I could afford to lose. What's more, I have several friends—guys like me, college graduates in their early thirties—who also lost money. Together, we are a new embarrassed group that I'm willing to bet is larger than you'd think.

How I lost money and what I lost it on came down to the same thing—technology. Using my computer, I invested in computer stocks. What happened to

[1]**bull market:** a situation in which the value of stocks is increasing.

(continued)

me could happen to you: the information superhighway ran me into the ground.

The beginning of my slide occurred when I stopped using my sleepy small-town stockbroker—the one who takes two-hour lunches and long fishing holidays—and started using a discount company offering round-the-clock access to the stock market, using the nearest touch-tone phone. My old broker got his tips from a Seattle firm known for its conservatism, and to me they were like the stock picks of a dead man: stocks in huge pharmaceutical companies and obscure Midwestern insurance companies. Boring. I wanted heat, adrenaline, action. I wanted to be, in some minor way, a player.

My first stock pick was Micron Technology (ticker symbol MU), a manufacturer of computer memory chips. I didn't read much information about the company (why waste precious nanoseconds?). I just picked up the phone and bought it. I don't remember the price, but it doesn't matter. What sank me wasn't buying the stock too high or selling it too low, but buying it and selling it and buying it and selling it: buying it when the price went down, selling it when the price went up, and then buying it back when the price went down again.

What breathless, baffling, futuristic days those were! CNBC, the cable business-news network, played constantly on my TV, my cordless phone was seldom out of reach, and my computer hummed, downloading graphs and numbers and reports onto my screen. Relaxing with my wife, I'd flip the tele-vision channels until CNBC flashed past with an MU quote. Excusing myself for coffee, I'd run to the phone to buy or sell stock, then return for an evening of stressful viewing.

Classic stupidity. Gambling addiction. Only myself to blame.

And blame myself I did. As other stock prices rose and rose, the value of my technology stocks fell, and my spirits sank. I was a loser and, judging by the financial page, the only one in the whole country. I suspected that my best friend was losing in the stock market, too, but whenever we spoke, his voice was upbeat. I probed him for a confession, but he resisted, and I was too ashamed to ask him if he, like me, had lost money. A coolness grew between us. Soon, we fell out of touch.

I thought about my father. He works as an attorney for a company that makes tape, glue, and sandpaper. I'd turned up my nose at the company's stock (too mundane), but he had loads of it. And it was soaring! By the time I decided to swallow my pride and buy in with him, I didn't have the funds.

My year of lousy investing made me wonder—about my own constitution, mostly. I wasn't cut out to be a risk taker, I'd learned, and probably never would be. When I'd set out to make a killing in the stock market, I hadn't realized that I might be the victim. Be my own stockbroker? Forget it! Let the experts have their ulcers, their long commutes into the city, and their rocky marriages. Me, I'm out of the game, and good riddance. I'm yanking out the wires. ◆

◆ SHARING YOUR TRUE STORIES

Discuss the answers to these questions with your classmates.

1. What were Walter Kirn's investment strategies? What were Anne Scheiber's investment strategies? How were they different? Do you know anyone who used Mr. Kirn's investment strategies? What was the result?

2. Re-read Walter Kirn's description of watching TV with his wife. What do you think she thought of his investment strategy? Do you think that men and women have different ideas about saving and investing money? How are they different? Do you have a story that demonstrates this?

3. Walter Kirn writes that investing in the stock market was not for him because he was not a risk taker. What about you? When it comes to investing money, are you a risk taker? Do you have a true story about a risk you've taken with money? Tell the class.

NEWS AND VIEWS

You have read about two people who invested in the stock market. Anne Scheiber made money; Walter Kirn lost money. Are there rules to follow when you invest in the stock market—rules that make it more likely that you will make money? The women in the photo believe there are rules, and they followed those rules carefully. Did they make money? In the following article, you will find out.

Before you read, look at the photo and think about the questions.

▸ Why do you think the women became interested in the stock market?

▸ Why are they standing around a statue of a bull? (Think of the title of the previous article.)

Chicks Laying Nest Eggs

1   Karin Housely, a young wife and mother, was worried about her family's financial future. Her husband earned a good salary, yet they never saved any money. How would they pay for their children's college educations? Would they have enough money in their retirement years? What would happen if her husband got sick or injured and couldn't work?

2   Karin learned that many of her friends had the same problem: Their families had no "nest eggs"—no money saved for the future. So, Karin invited nine friends to form an investment club, which they called the "Chicks Laying Nest Eggs Investment Club." First, the women learned all they could about saving and investing money. They concluded that the best way to invest money was to buy stocks in some good companies. They agreed that they would each contribute $50 every month and put their money together to buy stocks. They also agreed that they would not sell their stock for a long time—they would buy and hold. Then, years later, they would all have nest eggs.

3   On their Chicks Laying Nest Eggs Web site, the women describe the 12 investment strategies they use when buying stocks. They call these strategies "The Chicks' Dozen." Here, in the Chicks' own words, are four of their strategies:

1. Buy What You Know
by Cheryl

4   "Buy what you know" is my favorite tip. It's the only one of our principles that requires no research other than simply paying attention to your own life. Yipee! That I can do! Immediately, we are all transformed into expert stockpickers. "What?" you say. "Me? An expert? Already?" That's right. Open your refrigerator: What brand of ketchup do you buy? Soft drinks? Orange juice? Look in your pocket or purse: Which company made your cell phone? Go to the Internet: What is your favorite Web site? Start by looking at companies that are familiar to you—ones you know and love—and buy what you know.

5   Since this is the first step, I want to make sure you realize that buying what you know doesn't mean buying *everything* you know. This is simply the technique we use to get our list of stocks we will research.

2. K.I.S.S. (Keep it super simple.)
by Cheryl

6   If you are thinking about buying stock in a company, be sure you understand exactly what the company does. Peter Lynch (one of the most famous and successful investors) says you should be able to explain what a company does to a 10-year-old child and draw its product with a crayon. When you understand a company and its industry, you can more easily

predict whether its product or service is going to be in demand in the coming years.

3. Leader in Its Field
by Megan

7 Is the company the leader in its field? Would everyone recognize the name if you said it? To look for the top brands in an industry, name the first company that comes to your mind when you say, for example, "chocolate" or "fast-food restaurant" or "computer." These companies are all top dogs, leaders in their field. When you look for companies, look for the top dog. We don't want to invest in small start-up companies. They're too risky. We want the leaders in the field because they are established and proven.

4. Repeat Profitability
by Karin

8 How many times do you pick up the telephone each day? How many times do you turn on the lights? How many trips do you make to the gas station every month? How many soft drinks do you drink each week?

9 Repeaters are companies that have products that the consumer purchases often. For instance, I am addicted to Diet Coke. I have to have one Diet Coke a day . . . at noon. The Coca-Cola company must love me. Day in, day out, they can count on me coming back. Another example of a Repeater would be a pharmaceutical company. Just think of the millions of people who need to take some form of medication each day. I look at my Dad's medicine cabinet and I think he single-handedly keeps the pharmaceutical companies in business.

10 Why invest in a Repeater? The company has a greater opportunity to make a profit from its customer, over and over.

11 The other eight strategies are much more complicated; they include formulas that calculate, among other things, a company's gross margins, net margins, and cash flow ratio. The 10 women in the investment club learned what those financial terms mean, as well as how to use the formulas—an impressive accomplishment. But did they make money?

12 In 1998, the first year of the investment club, the women bought stocks in 10 U.S. companies. How did their stocks do compared with other stocks? From September 1998 to December 2000 the value of stocks in the 500 largest U.S. companies (the companies known as the "S&P 500") went up 8.16 percent. But the value of the stocks the women bought went up 17 percent.

13 The women claim that their main goal in forming the investment club was not to become millionaires, but to learn. Apparently they learned a lot. It will be interesting to see, years from now, just how big the Chicks' nest eggs are. ◆

BUILDING VOCABULARY

◆ UNDERSTANDING SPECIALIZED TERMS

The words below are from the stories "A Smart Investor" and "Chicks Laying Nest Eggs." Put each word in the right category. Write your answers on the lines.

top dog	stockholder	stock portfolio	stock certificates
investor	stockbroker	money manager	leader in its field
CEO	investments	leading company	investment strategy
consumer			

1. people

investor   _____

_____   _____

_____   _____

2. ways of describing a successful company

leading company   _____

_____

3. what a stockholder has

investment strategy   _____

_____   _____

DEVELOPING READING SKILLS

◆ UNDERSTANDING THE MAIN IDEAS

A reporter who interviewed Karin Housely asked the questions below. How do you think Karin Housely might have answered the questions? Write your answers on a separate piece of paper. The first one is done for you.

1. Your husband is a professional hockey player and earns a good salary, yet you were you worried about your family's financial future. Why?

   My husband was making a lot of money, but we weren't saving any of it. We spent every penny he made. So I was worried about the future. What if my husband got sick or injured and couldn't work? How would we pay for our children's educations? Would we have enough money when we retired? These were some of the things I was worried about.

2. Tell me a little about your investment club. Who's in it? How does it work?

3. How are your stocks doing so far?

◆ PARAPHRASING

Paraphrasing is expressing in your own words what someone has written or said, usually in a way that is shorter or clearer. Paraphrasing what you have read is a good way to check your comprehension. Also, re-reading your paraphrase is a good way to review before a test. You will find that it is not difficult to paraphrase material that you have understood well.

Re-read paragraphs 4–10 of "Chicks Laying Nest Eggs." In these paragraphs, the Chicks explain four of their investment strategies. Paraphrase the Chicks' explanations; that is, write them in your own words. Write your answers on a separate piece of paper.

1. Buy what you know. (paragraphs 4–5)

   If you are thinking about stocks, think first about companies that you like. Look around your home and notice which brands you buy—which toothpaste or soft drinks, for example. That doesn't mean that you go out and buy stocks in those companies. But it's a good way to get a list of possible companies to invest in.

2. Keep it super simple. (paragraph 6)

3. Leader in its field. (paragraph 7)

4. Repeat profitability. (paragraphs 8–10)

READING A BAR GRAPH

A **Read the following paragraph.**

Money managers admit that investing in the stock market has its risks; still, many say it is the best long-term investment in the United States—better than investing in bonds,[1] better than investing in gold, and certainly better than not investing money at all. They give the example of four people who each had $1,000 to invest in 1964. One person put the money under the mattress for safekeeping; one person bought gold; one person bought bonds; and one person bought stocks. This is how much money each person had in 1997, 33 years later:

▶ The person who put the money under a mattress still had $1,000 (although it would buy less than it did in 1964 because of inflation).

▶ The person who bought gold had $8,086.

▶ The person who bought bonds had $11,990.

▶ The person who bought stocks had $30,934.

---

[1] *Bonds* are pieces of paper you buy from a government (U.S. savings bonds, for example) or from a company. After a certain period of time, the government or company pays you back with interest. The longer the period of time, the higher the interest rate is.

B The information from the paragraph in Part A is represented in the bar graph below. Some information is missing from the graph. Read the paragraph again. Write the missing information in the box.

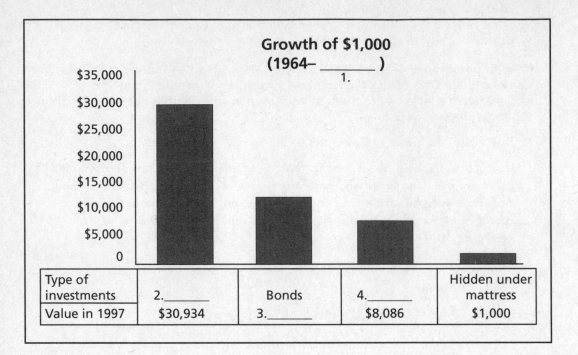

Growth of $1,000
(1964– _____)
1.

Type of investments	2._____	Bonds	4._____	Hidden under mattress
Value in 1997	$30,934	3._____	$8,086	$1,000

C Discuss your answers with your classmates.

1. The graph shows the growth of $1,000 from 1964 to 1997. Do you think the graph might look different if it showed the growth of $1,000 invested for a shorter period of time—for example, 1964 to 1969? How might it be different?

2. Is there another type of investment that you would like to see compared with the stock market in the graph? What is it?

3. Money managers admit that the stock market is not without its risks. If you had $1,000 to invest, would you take the risk of investing it in the stock market? Why or why not?

DISCUSSION

A The Chicks tell people to "buy what you know." Do you have any favorite brands? Are there brands you always buy, even though another brand is cheaper?

1. On a separate piece of paper, make a list of your five favorite brands. Show your list to a partner. Explain to your partner why you like these brands.

2. Sit with a partner. Tell your partner the name of the first company that comes to your mind when you hear the words below. Your partner will write your answers on the lines. Then discuss the question that follows.

car	_____	tea	_____
CD player	_____	coffee	_____
chocolate	_____	computer	_____
soft drink	_____	jeans	_____
detergent	_____	fast food	_____
toothpaste	_____	airline	_____
video game	_____		

▶ Did you and your classmates name any of the same companies? Do you think these companies are "top dogs"?

3. Pick three companies whose stock you would like to buy. Follow these steps to make your choices:

1. Using the Chicks' "buy what you know" rule, make a list of products that you and your classmates use or would like to use. Write your list on the board.

2. Using the Chicks' rules 2, 3, and 4, eliminate all but 10 products.

3. Find out which companies make the 10 products on your list.

4. Choose the three companies whose stock you would like to buy. (If you have access to the Internet, check the history of the companies you are interested in. Look for a graph that tells you if the stock price has been going up, going down, or going up and down. Use the information to narrow your list to three companies.)

5. Look in a newspaper or on the Internet to find out how much stock in your three companies costs per share. At a later date, check the price of your stocks.

B 1. Almost half of all families in the United States have money invested in the stock market. How do people in your country invest money? Tell the class.

2. Imagine that you have saved some money. You want to invest your money so that years from now you will have a nest egg. How would you invest your savings? Check (✓) the investment that makes the most sense to you. Then tell the class why you checked the investment you did.

❑ buy land or buildings

❑ buy gold

❑ buy foreign currency (German marks, Swiss francs, or U.S. dollars, for example)

❑ put the money in a savings account in a bank

❑ buy government bonds

❑ invest in the stock market

❑ invest in mutual funds (you buy stock in a group of companies that a mutual fund company chooses for you)

❑ _____

   (other)

WRITING

Choose one of the following topics to write about.

1. Do you know anyone who, like Anne Scheiber, invested money and became rich? Or do you know anyone who, like Walter Kirn, invested money and lost it? Write the story.

2. Anne Scheiber concluded that the surest way to get rich was to invest in stocks. What do you think is the surest way to get rich?

3. Research either the U.S. stock market crash of 1929 or the Great Depression that followed it. Write a report on what you learned.

4. The title of Anne Scheiber's story is "A Smart Investor." Do you think Anne Scheiber was smart? Explain your answer.

Helping One Another

In this unit, you will think about why people help one another. But first, you will think about times when people have helped you.

Use the questions below to interview a partner. Check (✓) your partner's answers. Then change roles. If you have a story you would like to share about a time you were helped, tell your partner.

Has anyone ever	Yes	No
1. loaned you money?	☐	☐
2. helped you change a flat tire?	☐	☐
3. helped you with your homework?	☐	☐
4. given you a ride home?	☐	☐
5. loaned you a tool?	☐	☐
6. loaned you a book?	☐	☐
7. loaned you some food?	☐	☐
8. given you directions when you were lost?	☐	☐
9. helped you move into a new home?	☐	☐
10. helped you find a job?	☐	☐
11. helped you make a difficult decision?	☐	☐
12. listened while you talked about your problems?	☐	☐

If you are like most people, you answered *yes* to many of the questions above, which means that people have helped you quite often in your life. Why do you think they helped you?

In this unit, you will first read the true story of a man whose life was saved by a stranger in World War II. Next, you will read the personal story of a young man who was surprised by a stranger's act of kindness. Finally, you will learn how most social psychologists in the West would answer the question, "Why do people help others?"

PRE-READING

Look at the photo and read the title of the story on the next page. With your classmates, make a list of questions you think the story will answer.

Example:

▶ *Is he a prisoner?*

▶ *What country is he from?*

When you have finished reading the story, look back at the questions you and your classmates wrote. Which questions did the story answer?

Chosen

1   In 1940, a year before the United States entered World War II, Irvin Scott volunteered for service in the U.S. Marines. He was 19 years old, six feet tall, and weighed 170 pounds. In 1945, when the war ended, he weighed 98 pounds, after spending almost the entire war as a prisoner of the Japanese. His survival was due partly to his own strength, both physical and mental, and partly to the kindness of two men—a Japanese guard and an American comrade.

2   After the war began, Scott was sent to the Bataan Peninsula in the Philippines. He was with a special radar unit that tried to detect incoming Japanese planes. Four months later, the Philippine islands were taken by the Japanese military, and Scott, along with thousands of other American servicemen, surrendered. Eventually, Scott was sent to Tayabas, a province on the island of Luzon in the Philippines. He and the other 300 American prisoners of war at Tayabas were ordered to finish building a road that the U.S. military had begun. Tayabas is located in the jungle, where heat, rain, and mosquitoes combine to make the conditions ideal for the spread of malaria. Over 100 of the 300 Americans died in the first three months at Tayabas. The prisoners who came down with malaria would lie outside on rocks in the pouring rain, seeking relief from their fevers.

3   Scott, too, came down with malaria, but remained strong enough to work. One day, he sat down to rest at the side of the road he was helping to build. In an attempt to keep his spirits up, he began to hum the aria "Un Bel Di" from the opera *Madame Butterfly,* his mother's favorite. As he sat at the roadside and hummed, Scott heard footsteps behind him and then a voice—the voice of a Japanese guard who said, "I know that song." The guard explained in English that when he was a teenager in Japan, he had worked for an American couple who had played "Un Bel Di" on a phonograph. *Madame Butterfly* had been their favorite opera, too. Scott never turned around as the guard spoke; guards and prisoners were not allowed to communicate, and Scott knew that if he and the guard were seen talking, both men's lives would be in danger. The guard finished speaking, and Scott heard the soft thud of something being dropped. When Scott turned around, the guard was gone. On the ground, there was a banana leaf wrapped around rice and a banana.

4   The Japanese guard was on duty every other day. Every time he was on duty, he managed to pass Scott, and, as he did, he dropped some food wrapped in a banana leaf. Apparently the guard was sharing his lunch with his American prisoner. The guard never spoke to Scott, and Scott never spoke to him. Scott never even learned the guard's name.

5   Several weeks later, Scott, whose malaria had worsened, passed out on the road he was working on. A fellow prisoner of war, Bill White, whom Scott did not know, carried him back to the camp—an act of heroism, as Bill White, like Scott, was sick and weak. Every few hours, White would carry Scott down to a creek to bathe him in cool water to try to bring his fever down. He fed him a mixture of rice and water the prisoners made, as well as the food the Japanese guard continued to drop at Scott's side. White also gave Scott quinine tablets for the malaria.

(continued)

6   At first, Scott was too delirious with fever to realize what he was being fed, but when he was stronger, he asked White where he had gotten the quinine tablets. White told Scott to wait until the afternoon, and to keep an eye on the guard.

7   Irvin Scott, who is now over 80 years old, remembers clearly what he saw that afternoon: "This Japanese guard came walking across the rocks. All the prisoners were lying out on the rocks, dying or barely able to move because of the malaria. As the guard passed by, he dropped something wrapped in a banana leaf. He kept walking and said nothing. Bill unwrapped the leaf, and in it was some rice and a little piece of paper. Inside the paper were two tablets of quinine."

8   With the help of Bill White and the food and quinine from the Japanese guard, Scott eventually regained some strength. He and Bill White were at Tayabas for the entire summer of 1942; then they were sent to a former American Army base near Manila that had been captured by the Japanese. They were there for about two years, and during that time Scott and White became close friends.

9   In 1944, Irvin Scott and Bill White were sent to Japan aboard separate ships. White's ship was sunk by torpedoes, but Scott's ship continued on to Japan. He worked in a coal mine there until the war ended in 1945 and then returned to the United States aboard a hospital ship.

10   From time to time, Scott thinks about Tayabas. He thinks about Bill White, who fed him the quinine tablets that the guard dropped. White had malaria, too, and no one would have known if he had swallowed the medicine instead of giving it to Scott. Scott also thinks about the Japanese guard. The two quinine tablets were half the guard's ration of four tablets, so the guard was risking dying of malaria himself. That, however, was the smaller risk: If the guard's superiors had seen him dropping the food and medicine, he would have been shot.

11   Scott can only speculate why, of all the prisoners at Tayabas, the guard chose to save him. "Who knows why he did it," Scott says. "I don't know to this day. He had to know something was wrong with what was happening. He had compassion, and I was the one he decided to help. I can only think it was because he heard me humming the melody 'Un Bel Di'."

12   The license plate on Scott's car says *P.O.W.*—prisoner of war. The license plate is a reminder of all the hardships Scott endured. Yet Scott does not hate the Japanese. On the contrary, he says the Japanese are "good human beings." What is the explanation for Scott's lack of hatred? Does he recognize that in war there is suffering on both sides—and that Japanese suffered at the hands of the Americans, just as he suffered at the hands of the Japanese? Perhaps he does. But there is also a simpler explanation: Scott finds it impossible to hate the Japanese because of the kindness and courage of one Japanese guard. Scott's car—the one with the *P.O.W.* license plate—is a Honda Accord. ◆

GETTING THE BIG PICTURE

Circle the letter of your answer.

Why is the story titled "Chosen"?

a. In 1940, Scott volunteered for service in the U.S Marines. Because he was strong both physically and mentally, he was chosen for a special radar unit.

b. Scott was a prisoner of war for four years. Because of all he endured, he has chosen not to talk about his experiences.

c. Of all the prisoners at the camp, the Japanese guard chose to save Scott. Because of the guard's help, Scott was able to survive the war.

BUILDING VOCABULARY

◆ RECALLING NEW WORDS

The words below are from the story. Write the correct answer on the line.

attempt	endured	managed to	speculates
delirious	keep an eye on	pass out	surrendered
due to	lack	relief	volunteered

1. In 1940, the United States was not yet at war, so American men did not have to be soldiers. Irvin Scott, however, wanted to be a soldier, so he _____ for service in the U.S. Marines.

2. Scott did not die because he was strong physically and mentally. His survival was also _____ the help of two men—a Japanese guard and an American comrade.

3. When the Japanese took the Philippines, U.S. soldiers put down their guns and stopped fighting. They _____ in 1941.

4. There were no doctors or medicine to help the sick prisoners; the only way they could find _____ from their fevers was to lie on the rocks when it rained.

5. Scott tried to stay mentally strong. In an _____ to keep his spirits up, he hummed his mother's favorite song.

6. It was dangerous and difficult for the Japanese guard to give food to Scott, but he succeeded in doing it. He _____ drop food every other day.

7. Scott fainted while working. Bill White saw him _____ and carried him back to camp.

8. When he was sick with malaria, Scott didn't know where he was or what was happening around him. Sometimes he thought he was home in his own bed; sometimes he saw his mother standing beside him. He was _____ with fever.

9. Scott watched the Japanese guard as he walked across the rocks because Bill White told him to _____ the guard.

10. Scott doesn't know why the guard chose to help him; he can only guess at the reason. He _____ the guard helped him because he was humming "Un Bel Di."

11. Scott suffered very much when he was a prisoner of war. His license plate, *P.O.W.*, is a reminder of all he _____.

12. Scott has no hatred for the Japanese. What is the explanation for his _____ of hatred?

◆ **USING NEW WORDS**

Complete the sentences with examples from your own life. In small groups, take turns reading your sentences aloud. Ask your classmates questions about their sentences.

1. To get relief when I am under a lot of stress, I _____.

2. I lack _____.

3. I would never attempt to _____.

4. Although it was difficult, I managed to _____.

5. I would volunteer immediately if someone asked for help with _____.

6. People sometimes pass out when _____.

DEVELOPING READING SKILLS

◆ **UNDERSTANDING THE MAIN IDEAS**

Complete the sentences. Circle the letter of the best answer.

1. This story is about an American prisoner of war
   a. who saved the lives of over 100 soldiers at a camp in the Philippines.
   b. whose life was saved by a Japanese guard and an American comrade.
   c. who died in the Philippines during the final month of World War II.

2. Irvin Scott was a prisoner of war
   a. for the entire summer of 1942.
   b. from 1941 to 1945.
   c. for several weeks in 1941.

3. The Japanese guard helped Scott by
    a. allowing him to escape.
    b. sending him to a hospital.
    c. dropping food and medicine.

4. Bill White helped Scott when he was sick by
    a. writing letters to his family.
    b. doing Scott's work for him.
    c. bathing him in cool water and giving him food and medicine.

5. Scott believes that the Japanese guard chose to save him because
    a. he liked Americans.
    b. he reminded him of an American man he had worked for.
    c. he heard him humming "Un Bel Di," a song that he knew.

6. Scott does not hate the Japanese because
    a. of the kindness and courage of the Japanese guard.
    b. many Japanese people helped him during the war.
    c. he lived with a Japanese couple when he was a teenager.

◆ IDENTIFYING TIME EXPRESSIONS

To show the passing of time, writers use time expressions. These time expressions tell you when events occured, how often they occured, or for how long they occured. The writer of "Chosen" uses many time expressions, such as "in 1944" and "four months later," to show the passing of time.

Complete the sentences below by matching each time expression with an event. Write the letter of your answer on the line.

Time Expression

1. In 1940, _____
2. In the first three months at Tayabas, _____
3. Every other day, _____
4. Eventually, _____
5. Until the war ended in 1945, _____
6. From time to time, _____

Event

a. Scott worked in a coal mine in Japan.
b. Scott thinks about Bill White and the Japanese guard.
c. Scott recovered from malaria and regained some strength.
d. the Japanese guard dropped food and medicine for Scott.
e. over 100 Americans died.
f. Irvin Scott volunteered for service in the U.S. Marines.

Sometimes writers do not state information directly. Then we have to use information they do give to make an *inference*—to make a logical guess. For example, the story does not tell us if Bill White survived the war. It does tell us, however, that his ship was sunk by torpedoes. So, we can infer that he did not survive the war, even though the writer does not state this directly.

The answers to the questions below are not in the story. Use the information you have to make a good guess.

1. In 1940, Irvin Scott weighed 170 pounds; in 1945, he weighed 98 pounds. What does that tell you about the amount of food he was given when he was a prisoner of war? *He probably did not get much food.*

2. The Japanese guard shared his lunch—some rice and a banana. What does that tell you about the food the Japanese soldiers in the Philippines had?_____

_____

3. If the guard's superiors had seen him dropping food, he would have been shot. What does that tell you about the character of the guard? _____

_____

4. Irvin Scott returned to the United States aboard a hospital ship. What does that tell you about his physical condition at that time? _____

_____

5. Why do you think Scott's humming "Un Bel Di" made the guard decide to save him?_____

_____

A PERSONAL STORY

People help one another in many ways, from life-saving acts to small, spontaneous acts of kindness.

Next you will read a story about an act of kindness. It is from a book titled *Earth Angels*. The book is a collection of true stories about ordinary people who helped others. A 17-year-old young man named Cesar told this story.

Look at the photo on page 141 and read the title of the story. Do you think Cesar helped someone? If so, how could he have helped someone? Or do you think someone helped Cesar? How could someone have helped him? Take a guess, and remember that no logical guess is wrong.

"Who Will Buy?" by Cesar from *Earth Angels*

There's someone special I want to tell you about. He's special because I don't know his name and I still can't figure out why he did what he did.

Have you ever seen those kids who stand out on the street corners selling flowers? Well, I'm one of them. A purple van filled with buckets of flowers picks me up near my apartment, then picks up a bunch of other kids, and drops us off at different street corners that are busy with traffic or near office buildings.

The man who drives the van is pretty tough. He has a system for counting money and the daily inventory of flowers. I guess because he's working with kids and has had some bad experiences, he has to watch us, so he doesn't get cheated. I don't take it personally when he asks me questions, but some of the kids don't like it much.

It's not as easy as you think to sell flowers. Our prices are good, better than at a flower store, but people are in a hurry and hardly see you standing there. A good day for me is when I sell 25 percent of everything I've got; that's a real good day.

You don't make much money, but it's better than some jobs. And I like being out in the open, by myself, watching the people.

Well, one day a man in his fifties or sixties was slowly walking up the sidewalk to my corner. I noticed him because he was wearing a bright colorful sweater that I couldn't help but see.

It took him a long time to get to my corner. I thought he would just keep walking, but he came right up to me, so I figured he wanted some flowers.

He said, "Young man, I've seen you many times at this spot and I've never seen anyone buy even one flower from you. Well, I'm gonna buy some flowers. How much?"

I told him the price for the daisies and the price for the roses.

"I want daisies and roses," he said, smiling at me sort of funny.

I grabbed one bunch of each. I liked him, so I picked out the best.

"No, no, no!" he said. "I want to buy every flower you've got."

I couldn't believe it. He took out an old leather wallet and pulled out lots and lots of money. He looked up at me and his smile got real big.

I was so nervous and excited, I didn't really know what to say. I just started to figure out how much it would cost to sell all the flowers I had.

(continued)

I began to gather them together, but then I realized that he couldn't carry them all. But I kept picking them up.

Then he put his hand on my arm to stop me and said, "Young man, I'll bet you have a girlfriend."

I said, "Her name is Ana; she lives on my block."

He said, "Tonight you will arrange your flowers on her doorstep."

He paid me more than the flowers cost and began walking slowly back down the sidewalk the same way he had come.

That was the one and only day I sold a hundred percent of the flowers. It's a day I'll always remember. ◆

◆ SHARING YOUR TRUE STORIES

Discuss the answers to these questions with your classmates.

1. Have you ever made a living selling things? What did you sell and where did you sell it? Cesar said a good day for him was when he sold 25 percent of what he had. What was a good day for you?

2. Read Cesar's description of the man who bought his flowers again. Do you think the man was rich? What are the clues that he was rich? What are the clues that he wasn't? In general, are rich people more likely to help others? If you have a story that supports your answer, tell it.

3. The authors of the book *Earth Angels* asked people to tell them stories about ordinary people who helped others. Cesar told the story of the man who bought all his flowers. If the authors asked you to tell them a story about someone who helped you, would you have a story to tell? Share it with the class.

4. With a partner, act out the scene in which the man buys all of the flowers. Do you have a true story about a stranger helping someone? Or can you imagine a scene in which a stranger helps someone? Act out that story, too.

5. Why do you think the man bought all of Cesar's flowers?

NEWS AND VIEWS

From time to time, Irvin Scott thinks about the Japanese guard who gave him food and medicine. "Who knows why he did it?" Scott asks. "I don't know to this day." And Cesar says of the man who bought all of his flowers, "I still can't figure out why he did what he did."

Why do people help one another? It is a question social psychologists—scholars who study the way people influence others' beliefs and behavior—have been asking for decades.

Before you read the article below, think about this statement:

People help other people because they want something in return.

Put an X on the line below near the word *agree* if you think the statement is true, near the word *disagree* if you think it is not true, and somewhere between the two words if your opinion is somewhere in between.

agree ————————————————————————— disagree

Where would most social psychologists in the West put their *X*? Read the article below to find out.

Helping Behavior

Why Do We Help Others?

1   Why do people help one another? Why do we stop to help a motorist change a flat tire? Why do we stay up all night comforting a friend? Why do we drop coins into a beggar's cup? Why do we give our money, time, possessions, and even our lives to others?

2   Some social psychologists have concluded that we give to other people because we get something in return. All helping acts, they say, ultimately help the helper. Sometimes the rewards for helping are external, and sometimes they are internal, but there are always rewards.

3   External rewards come from other people. We loan a classmate a pen, and she loans us a pen when we need one. We give the boss a ride in the hope of getting a promotion. We erase the blackboard for the teacher in the hope of getting a good grade. A wealthy couple gives money for cancer research and gets recognition.

4   Internal rewards are those we give ourselves. When we help others, we congratulate ourselves for being kind; we avoid feeling guilty or ashamed; and we relieve the distress we feel at seeing someone else in distress. Or perhaps helping others makes us feel superior to those we help, or it makes us feel connected to other people.

5   The idea that everyone's ultimate goal is to benefit himself or herself—even while helping others—is called egoism. It is the view held by the majority of social psychologists in the Western world. There is, however, a small minority of social psychologists who believe that sometimes people help others without wanting anything in return. This type of helping behavior is called altruism.

6   While social psychologists do not agree on what motivates people to help—egoism or altruism—they do agree that people are more likely to help under some circumstances and less likely to help under others.

When Do We Help Others?

7   **The bystander effect.** In 1964, people in the United States were shocked to hear about a young woman who had been stabbed to death in New York City. Thirty-eight people had witnessed the murder, and nobody had come to the woman's aid.

8   At 3 A.M. Kitty Genovese was walking home from work when a man caught and stabbed her. She screamed for help, and lights came on in several nearby apartments. Thirty-eight people saw the crime from their apartment windows, but only one person called the police, and the call came too late.

(continued)

9   People were shocked that no one had helped Kitty Genovese. Social psychologists, too, wondered why no one had helped. They speculated that no one helped *because* there were so many people around.

10   To test the theory that people in a group were less likely to help than a person alone, social psychologists did several experiments. One of the best-known experiments is called the "Lady in Distress."

11   In this experiment, a female experimenter asked college students to fill out a questionnaire. The experimenter left the room, saying she would return when the students had finished the questionnaire. Then the experimenter pretended that she had an accident in the next room. The students heard the sound of a chair being moved, followed by a loud scream and a crash. Next, they heard the woman crying and moaning, "Oh, my foot . . . I . . . can't move it. Oh . . . my ankle . . . I can't get this thing off me." The cries continued for about a minute and then stopped.

12   Would the students come to the woman's aid? When students were alone in the room, 70 percent of them went into the next room to see if the woman needed help. But when students were in the room with another student, only 20 percent offered help (Latané and Rodin, 1969).

13   The "Lady in Distress" experiment prompted social psychologists to come to this conclusion: As the number of bystanders (people who witness a crime or an accident) increases, offers of help decrease. This relationship between the number of bystanders and offers of help is called the "bystander effect."

Other factors that influence helping behavior. **14** Further experiments demonstrated that dozens of factors influence whether or not people help. For example, people are more likely to help when someone else helps first. Even the weather has an influence. (People are more likely to help on sunny days.) With so many factors affecting helping behavior, how can social psychologists predict with certainty when people will help? They cannot. They can only make general predictions about helping behavior. For example, social psychologists say the bystander effect holds true most of the time. So, if you are alone in a city and need help, ask a person standing alone rather than a person in a group.

Summary

For decades, social psychologists have been **15** studying helping behavior. They have been trying to answer primarily two questions:

1. Why do we help others? Some social **16** psychologists believe we help for selfish, egoistic reasons: Helping benefits us. Sometimes the reward is external, and sometimes it is internal, but there is always a reward for helping. Other social psychologists believe that sometimes we help for altruistic reasons, expecting no reward.

2. When do we help others? Generally **17** speaking, we are more likely to help others when we are alone than when we are with other bystanders. However, there are many other factors that affect helping behavior.

References

Latané, B., & Rodin, J. (1969) A lady in distress: Inhibiting effects of friends and strangers on bystander intervention. *Journal of Experimental Social Psychology* 5, 189–202. ◆

BUILDING VOCABULARY

◆ **UNDERSTANDING ACADEMIC VOCABULARY**

The words below are on the Academic Word List.* Find the words in "Helping Behavior" (The number in parentheses is the number of the paragraph.) If you are not sure what a word means, look it up in your dictionary. Then use the words in the sentences below.

concluded (2)	**benefit** (5)	**factors** (14)	**decade** (15)
external (2)	**circumstances** (6)	**predicted** (14)	**affected** (17)
goal (5)	**theory** (10)		

1. Rub the medicine on your face, but don't let any get into your mouth. The medicine is for _____ use only.

2. Unfortunately, they met when she was leaving and he was arriving; if _____ had been different, they might have become good friends.

3. His _____ is to be the owner of a small business by the time he is 30.

4. When she was a child, her grandfather _____ that she would be an actress someday, and he was right.

5. There are many _____ that influence the university's decision to admit a student; test scores and high school grades are only two of them.

6. When he moved from Mexico to Canada, he noticed that the long, dark winters _____ his mood; he sometimes became sad during the winter months.

7. After carefully comparing the two students' exams, the teacher _____ that one student must have copied the other student's answers.

8. Scientists in Great Britain thought that perhaps a million children jumping up and down at the same moment could cause a small earthquake. To test the _____, thousands of schoolchildren jumped up and down at 11 A.M. on September 7, 2001. (The jumping children did cause very small earthquakes.)

9. She decided to work in a hospital for a year before going to medical school because she thought she would _____ from the real-life experience.

10. In the United States, the _____ from 1920 to 1930 is called "The Roaring Twenties."

*For an explanation and the complete Academic Word List, see page 157.

◆ RECOGNIZING DEFINITIONS

In a textbook, there are many *terms*—words and expressions that are common in a particular field. These terms are often defined within the reading. As you read, it is important to recognize definitions. Here are three ways to recognize a definition in English:

▶ a dash before and after the definition (or sometimes only before the definition)

▶ a form of the verb *to be*

▶ the expression *is called*

Find these five terms—*social psychologists, egoism, altruism, internal rewards, external rewards,* and *the bystander effect*—on pages 142–144 and circle them. Notice how the writer of the article helps you recognize the definitions of these words.

Now look at the chart below. Some terms and definitions are missing. Fill in the missing information.

Terms	Definitions
_____ 1.	scholars who study the way people influence what others believe and what they do
_____ 2.	rewards that come from other people
internal rewards	_____ 3.
_____ 4.	the idea that everyone's ultimate goal in helping others is to benefit himself or herself
altruism	_____ 5.
_____ 6.	the relationship between the number of bystanders and offers of help

DEVELOPING READING SKILLS

◆ MAKING AN OUTLINE

Outlines can help you remember the main ideas and supporting details of a chapter in a textbook. Before a test, you can study your outline rather than study the textbook. Below is an informal outline a student might make after reading "Helping Behavior." Notice how the subheadings of the reading became part of the outline.

Some information is missing from the outline below. Complete the outline with information from the reading "Helping Behavior."

Helping Behavior

I. Why do we help others?

   A. Majority of social psychologists in the West: We help other people because we

     get something in _____. This idea is called _____.
                             1.   2.

     Two types of rewards for helping:

        1. External rewards come from other _____. Examples:
                                                          3.

           —Giving the boss a ride home to get a _____.
                                                   4.

           —Erasing the blackboard for the teacher to get a good _____.
                                                              5.

        2. _____ rewards—those we give ourselves. Examples:
                 6.

           —We _____ ourselves for being kind.
                  7.

           —We avoid feeling _____ or ashamed.
                            8.

   B. _____ of social psychologists: Sometimes people
       9.

     _____ others without wanting anything in return. This type
     10.

     of helping behavior is called _____.
                                            11.

II. When do we help others?

   A. The bystander _____: As the number of bystanders increases,
                       12.

     offers of help _____. Examples:
                  13.

        —The murder of Kitty Genovese in 1964

        —The "Lady in _____" experiment
                         14.

   B. Other factors that influence helping behavior:

        —Someone else helping first

        —Sunny _____
             15.

Social psychologists who were studying helping behavior did an experiment in the United States. They recorded the results of their experiment in the graph below. Read the graph.

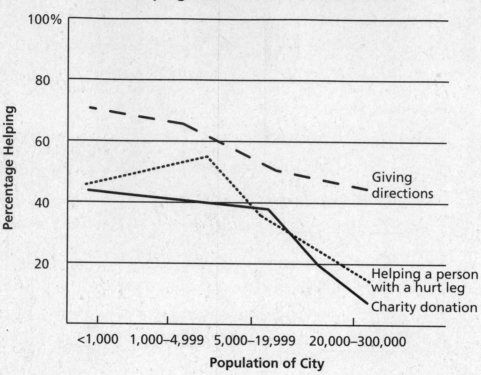

Helping Behavior in the United States

After studying the graph, discuss the answers to these questions with your classmates:

1. What do you think the psychologists wanted to learn from the experiment?

2. What were the results of the experiment?

3. Did the results of the experiment surprise you?

4. If you did the same experiment in your country, do you think the results would be the same?

DISCUSSION

A **Think about these questions. Discuss your answers with your classmates.**

1. The Japanese soldier risked his life for Scott. Can you think of other examples of people who risked their lives for strangers, perhaps during a war or during a time of persecution? Tell the class what you know about these people.

2. What possible rewards did the Japanese soldier and the man who bought Cesar's flowers get for helping?

3. Social psychologist C. Daniel Batson believes that altruism exists—that people sometimes help others without wanting anything in return. He believes his experiments prove that people will help for altruistic reasons when they think the person needing help is like them in some way. How do you think Dr. Batson would explain the behavior of the Japanese guard?

B **1.** **Below are three short news stories about people who helped others. Sit in groups of three. Choose one story and read it silently. Then summarize it for the other two people in your group.**

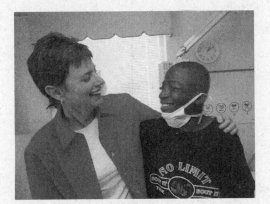

Jane Smith

Lenny Skutnik (in water)

Jane Smith is a teacher at a middle school in the United States. A student at the school, a 13-year-old boy, was very ill with kidney disease. His kidneys had stopped functioning, and he was having dialysis treatments three times a week. Ms. Smith, who is married and the mother of a son, offered to give the boy one of her kidneys, and he and his family accepted her offer. At a hospital in North Carolina, doctors removed Mrs. Smith's kidney and placed it in the boy. The donated kidney is working well, and the boy is no longer on dialysis. The teacher is doing fine, too.

In January 1982, a plane taking off from Washington, D.C., crashed into the Potomac River. The survivors of the crash were in the icy water, and helicopters were lowering ropes to them. One of the survivors, a young woman, was too weak to hang on to the rope. Three times she grabbed the rope but fell back into the water. A small crowd of people were watching the rescue attempt from the banks of the river. Suddenly a man named Lenny Skutnik ran out of the crowd, swam through chunks of ice to the woman, and rescued her. Both he and the young woman survived.

Keshia Thomas

Fifteen members of the Ku Klux Klan, a small, extremist group that promotes hatred toward certain races and religious groups, were marching through the streets of Ann Arbor, Michigan. One thousand people who opposed the group came to shout at them. Suddenly, some people in the group of 1,000 began beating one of the Ku Klux Klan members. Keshia Thomas, an 18-year-old African American woman, fell on top of the man who was being beaten and shielded him with her body. The man survived and had only minor injuries.

2. Now think about these questions. Discuss your answers with your classmates.

1. What possible external or internal rewards could Jane Smith, Lenny Skutnik, and Keshia Thomas have gotten from helping?

2. Do the actions of Lenny Skutnik and Keshia Thomas support the "bystander effect"? Explain your answer.

3. Do any of these stories remind you of a similar story? Tell your story to the class.

WRITING

Choose one of the following topics to write about.

A Irvin Scott, the prisoner of war, and Cesar, the flower seller, were helped by strangers. Most of the time, though, help comes not from strangers but from people we know well—from parents, sisters, brothers, friends, neighbors, and teachers.

1. Read the lyrics to the song "Because You Loved Me," which Celine Dion recorded. If possible, listen to a recording of the song as you read.

> **Because You Loved Me**
> For all those times you stood by me
> For all the truth that you made me see
> For all the joy you brought to my life
> For all the wrong that you made right
> For every dream you made come true
> For all the love I found in you
> I'll be forever thankful, baby

You're the one who held me up
Never let me fall
You're the one who saw me through—through it all
    You were my strength when I was weak
    You were my voice when I couldn't speak
    You were my eyes when I couldn't see
    You saw the best there was in me
    Lifted me up when I couldn't reach
    You gave me faith 'cause you believed
    I'm everything I am
    Because you loved me.
You gave me wings and made me fly
You touched my hand, I could touch the sky
I lost my faith, you gave it back to me
You said no star was out of reach
You stood by me and I stood tall
I had your love, I had it all
Maybe I don't know that much
But I know this much is true
I was blessed because I was loved by you
  You were my strength . . .
You were always there for me
The tender wind that carried me
A light in the dark shining your love into my life
You've been my inspiration
Through the lies you were the truth
My world is a better place because of you
    You were my strength . . .

2. **Write a short essay about a person who helped you. For example, did this person**

▶ make your dream come true?

▶ give you strength when you were weak?

▶ say no star was out of reach?

▶ inspire you?

B **What are some volunteer organizations in your community? Find out what one of the organizations does and summarize the information in a report. You can also interview someone who volunteers at the organization. Find out what they do and why they do it. Write a report on what you learned.**

Appendix 1

Life Expectancies Around the World

COUNTRY	MALES	FEMALES	AVERAGE*
Argentina	72	79	76
Brazil	59	68	64
Czech Republic	71	78	75
China	70	73	72
Colombia	67	75	71
Dominican Republic	71	76	74
France	75	83	79
Germany	74	81	78
Greece	76	81	79
Guatemala	64	69	67
Hong Kong	77	82	80
Hungary	67	76	72
Italy	76	82	79
Japan	78	84	81
Mexico	68	75	72
Nepal	58	57	58
Nigeria	52	52	52
Pakistan	60	62	61
Poland	69	78	74
Russia	62	73	68
Somalia	45	48	47
South Korea	71	79	75
Spain	75	82	79
Thailand	65	72	69
United States	74	80	77
World	**62**	**65**	**64**

If the life-expectancy figures for your native country are not in the chart above, you can find them in the *World Almanac* or on the Web site of the CIA, the U.S. Central Intelligence Agency at *www.cia.gov*.

* Figures have been rounded up to next whole number.

Appendix 2

Checking Your Answers

Unit 1

Pre-Reading (page 2)

The man in the photo is 94 years old.

Discussion (pages 16–17)

STEPS		STARS
1.	Don't overdo alcohol.	★★★★★
2.	Don't use illegal drugs, like heroin or cocaine.	★★★★★
3.	Eat more fruits and vegetables–five to seven per day	★★★★★
4.	Cut the amount of fat in your diet.	★★★★★
5.	Fasten seat belts.	★★★★
6.	Take an aspirin every day.	★★★★★
7.	Get enough sleep.	★★★
8.	Take care of your teeth and gums.	★★★
9.	Have a sense of humor.	★★★★
10.	Build good relationships with friends.	★★★★
11.	Own a pet.	★★
12.	Make your workplace fun.	★★★

Unit 2

A Personal Story (page 26)

The two professions Ruth Reichl chose were restaurant critic and editor of a magazine about food.

Unit 3

Pre-Reading (page 37)

• My computer suddenly stopped working.

• I work for a small, new company that does business on the Internet.

• I sit at my computer for a couple of hours every evening, looking for places on the Internet that interest me.

Discussion (page 54)

A 1. **True.** For example: In 1995, at Carnegie Mellon University in Pittsburgh, only 8 percent of the computer science majors were female. In 2000, 40 percent of the computer science majors were female.

2. **True.** In a newspaper interview, one Internet entrepreneur said he was making $175,000 a year but lived in an apartment with no furniture because he didn't have time to shop. Geeks say that working 60–80 hours a week is not unusual.

3. **False.** A recent study showed that geeks watch more TV than the rest of the population. They watch 6 percent more prime-time television and 21 percent more late-night TV than people who do not use the Internet. The study also showed that Net users watch more movies and listen to more radio, too.

4. **True.** A company in Silicon Valley offers a course in etiquette, called "Workshoppe," for geeks. The course costs $150, and the first class is in a restaurant.

5. **True.** Some large cruise ship lines, like Holland America, offer special cruises for geeks, with courses like "Using the Perl DBI." The Geek Cruises are about $750 more expensive than a regular one-week cruise.

6. **True.** There is a volunteer organization called "Geekcorps." Their motto is: "Together, we can make sure the World Wide Web includes the whole wide world."

C 1. the moment in which you realize you've made a major computer mistake

2. communicating by actually walking to a person's office and speaking with him or her (instead of communicating by e-mail or voice mail)

3. images on a computer screen that are attractive to look at

4. printed magazines and newspapers

5. a program that can spread quickly from one computer to millions of others around the world

6. the average work week in technology fields: 24 hours a day, 7 days a week

Unit 4

Discussion (page 75)

B 2. Tom got letters and e-mail from people all over the world. (Some women wrote him that they looked exactly like the woman in the picture. The problem was that they were already married.) He spent thousands of dollars and drove thousands of miles to meet women who looked like his "dream girl." He met a lot of women but, after talking with them, decided they were not his soul mate. He is still looking for her.

Unit 5

Discussion (page 95)

B 2. Craig Karges says there is no magic in the way the pendulum works; you are making the pendulum swing. He explains with this example: "Imagine you're driving down the highway and you're late for an appointment. You think to yourself, 'I'm going to be really late, I've got to get there.' All of a sudden you look at your speedometer and see you're going 80 miles an hour. Your subconscious mind is saying, 'We have to get there! Step on it!' You don't consciously feel yourself putting extra pressure on the gas pedal, but you are. Your subconscious mind is sending a message down to your foot, and your foot presses down on the gas pedal." The pendulum works the same way: Your subconscious mind, where your intuition is buried, sends a signal to your body to control the swinging of the pendulum.

Unit 6

Discussion (page 113)

B 1. The bratwurst feud went to Germany's highest court. The court ruled that the man could grill sausages only five times each summer.

2. Neighbors and the church fought over the soup kitchen for five years. Finally, the case went to court. The judge said the kitchen could open. The day the kitchen opened, 150 people came for a free breakfast, ate quietly, and left. There were no problems.

3. Neighbors tried for 15 years to get the woman to clean up her yard. Finally, the neighbors decided to sue her for the emotional harm looking at the junk was causing them. The judge awarded the neighbors $114,000. The woman refused to pay and was sentenced to 30 days in jail. She disappeared, and the city sold her house. The new owners found two to three feet of trash in every room and piles of garbage on every bed.

4. Neighbors complained to their city's planning commission. The planning commission asked the billionaire to meet with his neighbors and a mediator. The billionaire promised to limit construction hours and complete the house within one year.

5. The problem with the parrot was never really resolved. The neighbors complained at City Hall, and an official there found a law that forbids anyone from "allowing any animal or bird to make loud noises." The city asked Bubba's owner to keep Bubba inside. She refused. The feud between Bubba's owner and the neighbors continued for two years. Finally, the neighbors who complained the most about Bubba moved. Bubba is still on the balcony and has become a TV star.

Unit 7

Pre-Reading (page 115)

KEY TO SYMBOLS	
52-week high	the highest price the stock sold for during the past year
Low	the lowest price the stock sold for during the past year
Stock	stock exchange abbreviation (the ticker symbol) of the name of the company
Div	annual dividend
PE	stock price divided by per-share earnings in the past year
Last	final trading price on the previous day
Change	change in price from the previous day

Appendix 3

Academic Word List

The Academic Word List is a list of 570 words that are commonly found in textbooks written in English. If you are studying in an English-speaking country, it is important to know these words.

The Academic Word List is divided into 10 sublists, with Sublist 1 containing the most frequent words and Sublist 10 the least frequent in the list. The numbers indicate the sublist that the words belong to (e.g., *abandon* and its family members are in Sublist 8).

abandon	8	assess	1	comment	3
abstract	6	assign	6	commission	2
academy	5	assist	2	commit	4
access	4	assume	1	commodity	8
accommodate	9	assure	9	communicate	4
accompany	8	attach	6	community	2
accumulate	8	attain	9	compatible	9
accurate	6	attitude	4	compensate	3
achieve	2	attribute	4	compile	10
acknowledge	6	author	6	complement	8
acquire	2	authority	1	complex	2
adapt	7	automate	8	component	3
adequate	4	available	1	compound	5
adjacent	10	aware	5	comprehensive	7
adjust	5	behalf	9	comprise	7
administrate	2	benefit	1	compute	2
adult	7	bias	8	conceive	10
advocate	7	bond	6	concentrate	4
affect	2	brief	6	concept	1
aggregate	6	bulk	9	conclude	2
aid	7	capable	6	concurrent	9
albeit	10	capacity	5	conduct	2
allocate	6	category	2	confer	4
alter	5	cease	9	confine	9
alternative	3	challenge	5	confirm	7
ambiguous	8	channel	7	conflict	5
amend	5	chapter	2	conform	8
analogy	9	chart	8	consent	3
analyze	1	chemical	7	consequent	2
annual	4	circumstance	3	considerable	3
anticipate	9	cite	6	consist	1
apparent	4	civil	4	constant	3
append	8	clarify	8	constitute	1
appreciate	8	classic	7	constrain	3
approach	1	clause	5	construct	2
appropriate	2	code	4	consult	5
approximate	4	coherent	9	consume	2
arbitrary	8	coincide	9	contact	5
area	1	collapse	10	contemporary	8
aspect	2	colleague	10	context	1
assemble	10	commence	9	contract	1

contradict	8	draft	5	focus	2
contrary	7	drama	8	format	9
contrast	4	duration	9	formula	1
contribute	3	dynamic	7	forthcoming	10
controversy	9	economy	1	found	9
convene	3	edit	6	foundation	7
converse	9	element	2	framework	3
convert	7	eliminate	7	function	1
convince	10	emerge	4	fund	3
cooperate	6	emphasis	3	fundamental	5
coordinate	3	empirical	7	furthermore	6
core	3	enable	5	gender	6
corporate	3	encounter	10	generate	5
correspond	3	energy	5	generation	5
couple	7	enforce	5	globe	7
create	1	enhance	6	goal	4
credit	2	enormous	10	grade	7
criteria	3	ensure	3	grant	4
crucial	8	entity	5	guarantee	7
culture	2	environment	1	guideline	8
currency	8	equate	2	hence	4
cycle	4	equip	7	hierarchy	7
data	1	equivalent	5	highlight	8
debate	4	erode	9	hypothesis	4
decade	7	error	4	identical	7
decline	5	establish	1	identify	1
deduce	3	estate	6	ideology	7
define	1	estimate	1	ignorance	6
definite	7	ethic	9	illustrate	3
demonstrate	3	ethnic	4	image	5
denote	8	evaluate	2	immigrate	3
deny	7	eventual	8	impact	2
depress	10	evident	1	implement	4
derive	1	evolve	5	implicate	4
design	2	exceed	6	implicit	8
despite	4	exclude	3	imply	3
detect	8	exhibit	8	impose	4
deviate	8	expand	5	incentive	6
device	9	expert	6	incidence	6
devote	9	explicit	6	incline	10
differentiate	7	exploit	8	income	1
dimension	4	export	1	incorporate	6
diminish	9	expose	5	index	6
discrete	5	external	5	indicate	1
discriminate	6	extract	7	individual	1
displace	8	facilitate	5	induce	8
display	6	factor	1	inevitable	8
dispose	7	feature	2	infer	7
distinct	2	federal	6	infrastructure	8
distort	9	fee	6	inherent	9
distribute	1	file	7	inhibit	6
diverse	6	final	2	initial	3
document	3	finance	1	initiate	6
domain	6	finite	7	injure	2
domestic	4	flexible	6	innovate	7
dominate	3	fluctuate	8	input	6

Academic Word List

insert	7	military	9	pose	10
insight	9	minimal	9	positive	2
inspect	8	minimize	8	potential	2
instance	3	minimum	6	practitioner	8
institute	2	ministry	6	precede	6
instruct	6	minor	3	precise	5
integral	9	mode	7	predict	4
integrate	4	modify	5	predominant	8
integrity	10	monitor	5	preliminary	9
intelligence	6	motive	6	presume	6
intense	8	mutual	9	previous	2
interact	3	negate	3	primary	2
intermediate	9	network	5	prime	5
internal	4	neutral	6	principal	4
interpret	1	nevertheless	6	principle	1
interval	6	nonetheless	10	prior	4
intervene	7	norm	9	priority	7
intrinsic	10	normal	2	proceed	1
invest	2	notion	5	process	1
investigate	4	notwithstanding	10	professional	4
invoke	10	nuclear	8	prohibit	7
involve	1	objective	5	project	4
isolate	7	obtain	2	promote	4
issue	1	obvious	4	proportion	3
item	2	occupy	4	prospect	8
job	4	occur	1	protocol	9
journal	2	odd	10	psychology	5
justify	3	offset	8	publication	7
label	4	ongoing	10	publish	3
labor	1	option	4	purchase	2
layer	3	orient	5	pursue	5
lecture	6	outcome	3	qualitative	9
legal	1	output	4	quote	7
legislate	1	overall	4	radical	8
levy	10	overlap	9	random	8
liberal	5	overseas	6	range	2
license	5	panel	10	ratio	5
likewise	10	paradigm	7	rational	6
link	3	paragraph	8	react	3
locate	3	parallel	4	recover	6
logic	5	parameter	4	refine	9
maintain	2	participate	2	regime	4
major	1	partner	3	region	2
manipulate	8	passive	9	register	3
manual	9	perceive	2	regulate	2
margin	5	percent	1	reinforce	8
mature	9	period	1	reject	5
maximize	3	persist	10	relax	9
mechanism	4	perspective	5	release	7
media	7	phase	4	relevant	2
mediate	9	phenomenon	7	reluctance	10
medical	5	philosophy	3	rely	3
medium	9	physical	3	remove	3
mental	5	plus	8	require	1
method	1	policy	1	research	1
migrate	6	portion	9	reside	2

resolve	4	specify	3	theory	1
resource	2	sphere	9	thereby	8
respond	1	stable	5	thesis	7
restore	8	statistic	4	topic	7
restrain	9	status	4	trace	6
restrict	2	straightforward	10	tradition	2
retain	4	strategy	2	transfer	2
reveal	6	stress	4	transform	6
revenue	5	structure	1	transit	5
reverse	7	style	5	transmit	7
revise	8	submit	7	transport	6
revolution	9	subordinate	9	trend	5
rigid	9	subsequent	4	trigger	9
role	1	subsidy	6	ultimate	7
route	9	substitute	5	undergo	10
scenario	9	successor	7	underlie	6
schedule	8	sufficient	3	undertake	4
scheme	3	sum	4	uniform	8
scope	6	summary	4	unify	9
section	1	supplement	9	unique	7
sector	1	survey	2	utilize	6
secure	2	survive	7	valid	3
seek	2	suspend	9	vary	1
select	2	sustain	5	vehicle	8
sequence	3	symbol	5	version	5
series	4	tape	6	via	8
sex	3	target	5	violate	9
shift	3	task	3	virtual	8
significant	1	team	9	visible	7
similar	1	technical	3	vision	9
simulate	7	technique	3	visual	8
site	2	technology	3	volume	3
so-called	10	temporary	9	voluntary	7
sole	7	tense	8	welfare	5
somewhat	7	terminate	8	whereas	5
source	1	text	2	whereby	10
specific	1	theme	8	widespread	8

Academic Word List

Text Credits

Pages 9–10, reprinted with permission from *Having Our Say* by Sarah and Elizabeth Delany with Amy Hill Hearth, published by Kodansha America, Inc. Copyright © 1993.

Pages 11–12, from *The Longevity Code* by Zorba Paster and Susan Meltsner, copyright © 2001 by Zorba Paster. Used by permission of Clarkson Potter/Publishers, a division of Random House, Inc.

Page 16, the life expectancy figures are from the Web site of the CIA, the U.S. Central Intelligence Agency, at *www.cia.gov*.

Page 19, the ten factors people consider when choosing work were drawn from a list in *Discover What You're Best At* by Linda Gale, A Fireside Book (Simon and Schuster), New York, 1998.

Pages 21–22, the quotes from the firefighters are from a transcript of Stone Phillips's *Dateline NBC* interview on 28 September 2001.

Pages 26–27, from *Tender at the Bone* by Ruth Reichl, copyright © 1998 by Ruth Reichl. Used by permission of Random House, Inc.

Pages 28–29, the ideas presented in "Becoming Yourself" are those of Parker Palmer. The quote is from his book *Let Your Life Speak* by Parker Palmer, copyright © 1999. Reprinted by permission of John Wiley and Sons.

Page 34, the list of the top 15 jobs is consolidated from a list in *Best Jobs for the 21st Century* by J. Michael Farr and LaVerne Ludden, JIST Works, Inc., Indianapolis, 1999. The authors based their recommendations on statistics compiled by the U.S. Department of Labor.

Pages 45–46, "Calm in Crisis Is in My Blood" is from the *New York Times*, 14 March 2001. Copyright © 2001 by the New York Times Co. Reprinted by permission.

Pages 47–48, from *Geeks* by Jon Katz, copyright © 2000 by Jon Katz. Used by permission of Villard Books, a division of Random House, Inc.

Pages 59–60, "Shipmates and Soul Mates" by Elizabeth Leland was originally published under the title "New Love, 2 by 2" in the *Charlotte Observer*, 6 June 1999. Reprinted by permission of the author.

Pages 65–66, the four responses to the question "What are you looking for in a spouse?" were excerpted from interviews recorded at the University of Wisconsin, Whitewater, in 2002.

Pages 67–68, the information in "Who Wants to Marry a Soul Mate?" is from "Who Wants To Marry a Soul Mate?" by Barbara Dafoe Whitehead and David Popnoe, from the National Marriage Project's 2001 Report.

Pages 67–68, from "Marriage, 20-Something Style" by Hayley Kaufman, the *Boston Globe*, 24 June 2001. Copyright © by The Boston Globe. Reprinted by permission of the Boston Globe via the Copyright Clearance Center.

Page 72, the statements are adapted from the survey conducted by Barbara Dafoe Whitehead and David Popnoe as part of the National Marriage Project.

Page 75, "Have you seen this girl?" is reprinted by permission of Tom Kraemer and Bob Pagani. Copyright 2002 Bob Pagani.

Page 76, the "helpful questions to get you started" in the writing prompt are reprinted by permission of Match.com.

Page 77, the intuition quiz was adapted from the one designed by Bill Kautz and the staff at the Center of Applied Intuition in Fairfax, CA.

Pages 79–80, the story "A Sixth Sense" is based on Kathy Passero's account in *Biography*, November 2000.

Pages 85–86, "A Parent's Sixth Sense" is reprinted from *Parents*, July 2000. Copyright © 2000 Gruner and Jahr USA Publishing. Reprinted from *Parents* by permission.

Pages 87–88, much of the information in "When Not to Use Your Head" is from Paul Bagne's article "When to Follow a Hunch," in *Reader's Digest*, May 1994.

Pages 92–93, the information in the chart is from Bill Taggart's Web site, "The Intuitive Self".

Page 94, the pendulum technique is from *Ignite Your Intuition* by Craig Karges, Health Communications, Inc., Deerfield Beach, FL, 1999.

Page 95, the statements about intuition are from the Web site of the Center of Applied Intuition in Fairfax, CA.

Pages 99–100, The story "Family Feud" is based on the account of historian Altina Waller, author of *Feud: Hatfields, McCoys, and Social Change in Appalachia, 1860–1900,* University of North Carolina Press, 1989.

Pages 105–106, "Corn" is reprinted by permission of Frances Collin, Literary Agent. Copyright © 1975 by Ben T. Logan.

Pages 107–108, "Neighborhood Feuds" was excerpted from "The Neighbors from Hell" by Mark Stuart Gill, Copyright June 1994, Meredith Corporation. All rights reserved. Used with the permission of *Ladies Home Journal.*

Page 112, the "Top Seven Causes of Neighborhood Feuds" were supplied by Shelley Whalen, Executive Director of Community Mediation Services of Central Ohio. Ms. Whalen has been mediating disputes for 13 years.

Pages 117–118, the story "A Smart Investor" is based on "Death and the Maven" by Sharon Epperson in *Time,* 18 December 1995.

Pages 123–124, "How I Lost Money in the Bull Market" by Walter Kirn is reprinted by permission of the author. The article is from the *New York Times,* 11 February 1996.

Pages 126–127, the Chicks' four rules are reprinted by permission of International Creative Management, Inc. Copyright © 2001 by Karin Housely.

Pages 141–142, from *Earth Angels* by Jerry Biederman and Lorin Biederman, Copyright © 1997 by Jerry Biederman and Lorin Biederman. Used by permission of Broadway Books, a division of Random House, Inc.

Pages 143–144, The information in "Helping Behavior" is from *The Altruism Question: Toward a Social-Psychological Answer* by C. Daniel Batson, Lawrence Erlbaum Associates, 1991.

Page 148, The statistics in the graph are from the research of P. Amato (1993) "Helping behavior in urban and rural environments." *Journal of Personality and Social Psychology,* 45, 571–586.

Pages 150–151, "Because You Loved Me" by Diane Warren © Realsongs (ASCAP) and Touchstone Pictures Songs & Music, Inc. (ASCAP) All rights reserved. Used by permission Warner Bros. Publications U.S. Inc., Miami, FL 33014.

Many of the definitions used in the vocabulary exercises are from the *Longman Advanced American Dictionary,* © Pearson Education, 2000.

The Academic Word List was compiled by Averil Coxhead, School of Linguistics and Applied Language Studies, Victoria University of Wellington, New Zealand. For more information about the list, see "A New Academic Word List" in the *TESOL Quarterly,* 34(2): 213–238. The complete list is also on the Internet. Searching under "Academic Word List" or "Averil Coxhead" will take you to the list.

The three-step preparation for writing recommended in the To the Teacher section is from the research of Elizabeth Stolarek ("Prose Modeling and Metacognition: The Effect of Modeling on Developing a Metacognitive Stance toward Writing" in *Research in the Teaching of English,* Vol. 28, No. 2, May 1994).

Text Credits

Photo Credits